ANSWERING THE TOUGHEST QUESTIONS ABOUT SUFFERING AND EVIL

ANSWERING THE TOUGHEST QUESTIONS ABOUT SUFFERING AND EVIL

BRUCE BICKEL & STAN JANTZ

WITH CHRISTOPHER GREER

BETHANYHOUSE

a division of Baker Publishing Group
Minneapolis, Minnesota

Published by Bethany House Publishers
11400 Hampshire Avenue South
Bloomington, Minnesota 55438
www.bethanyhouse.com

Bethany House Publishers is a division of
Baker Publishing Group, Grand Rapids, Michigan

Printed in the United States of America

Library of Congress Control Number: 2017936765

ISBN 978-0-7642-1872-9

Cover design by Rob Williams, InsideOutCreativeArts

Authors are represented by The Steve Laube Agency

17   18   19   20   21   22   23   7   6   5   4   3   2   1

Contents

Acknowledgments

Bruce and Stan want to thank Christopher Greer for the work he contributed to this book. In addition to conducting countless personal interviews and designing the surveys, he helped outline and write several chapters.

Bruce, Stan, and Chris want to acknowledge the hundreds of young adults—especially those from St. Andrew's Presbyterian Church in Newport Beach, California—who took the time to articulate their most important questions about suffering and evil. The questions you asked show that you really want to know.

Introduction

When we started doing research for the book you are holding, most of the material that gave us inspiration came from books considered modern "classics." Esteemed writers such as C. S. Lewis, R. C. Sproul, Philip Yancey, and Peter Kreeft have crafted helpful books out of their encounters with pain and suffering, whether in their own lives or through the experiences of others. Books such as *The Problem of Evil*, *Where Is God When It Hurts?*, and *Surprised by Suffering* have helped many people come to grips with the suffering and evil in our world and in their lives.

Added to these classics is a surge of contemporary books on the topic—including this one. It seems as though a lot of people are suffering and dying these days, and they are eager to write about what they have learned. A recent number-one *New York Times* bestselling book by a world-renowned neurosurgeon is endorsed by a bestselling novelist who assures us that we will "both mourn his death and benefit from his life." A video posted by a famous country singer about a high school teacher dying from cancer has been viewed more than twenty-five million times.

As morbid as this sounds, we have to ask the question: Why have suffering and death suddenly become popular? It's not as if these are new topics, suddenly thrust upon us like the latest fashion trend. Suffering and evil and dying and death have been with us since near the beginning of the human race. Why the interest now?

Until recently, the topics of death and suffering and the evil that gets tied up in the mix haven't been in demand, and it's not hard to see why. Reading a book isn't a high priority for people in the middle of some deep pain and loss. For those who live pretty comfortable lives except for periodic setbacks and the occasional bout of suffering, why read a book about suffering and evil if you don't have to?

That's the way it used to be, but not anymore. Evil on a global scale and the suffering it produces have been brought to our doorstep through the devices that live in our pockets. People being martyred for their faith, refugees stacked up like cordwood in deplorable conditions, children starving and dying of diseases—we used to be able to hold these realities at arm's length, but now they assault our senses through stark images made possible by the ever-present media.

Besides the presence of suffering and evil "out there" that we all must contend with, most of us are dealing with problems of our own. Or we are experiencing the negative effects of disease or hardship through family and friends. Regardless of our perspective, we are encountering suffering and evil in one form or another almost every day of our lives. It's more than most of us can handle on our own, so we are increasingly looking for answers, reasons, and solutions for all the bad stuff in the world.

This is precisely the reason we wrote this book. We needed answers to the questions about suffering and evil we have been asking for a very long time. As we did for *Answering the Toughest Questions About God and the Bible* and *Answering the Toughest Questions About Heaven and Hell*, the first two books in this series, we didn't rely only on our own questions. With the help of Christopher Greer, a pastor who ministers primarily to young adults, we compiled a list of questions asked by people a lot like you. We then selected the ten that best represented the questions people like you are asking. From there we did our research by reading dozens of books and hundreds of articles and by talking to many people about their own experiences with suffering and evil.

Even though there are a lot of resources available, this was a difficult book to write. We think there are three reasons for this:

1. *There are no easy answers to the problem of suffering and evil.* This is a complex topic that touches all of us in one way or another, yet there aren't always clear-cut solutions. In fact, easy answers are pretty rare.
2. *We don't always understand God's ways.* How we would love for God to directly answer our cries for help when the going gets tough, or at least to give us a blueprint in his Word, the Bible. But that just isn't the case.
3. *Suffering can be beneficial.* We talk a lot about paradoxes in the book, and this is one of them: Good can come from bad. Nobody asks for afflictions or troubles to come their way, but after they subside, almost nobody regrets that they happened.

Despite these challenges—or perhaps because of them—we think the book you are holding offers a helpful perspective on suffering and evil and how God relates to both. We have done our best to provide answers to your toughest questions, but that's not the end of it. Throughout the book we ask you questions. These aren't rhetorical questions (remember, there are no easy answers). Instead, the questions are designed to prompt your thinking and stir your imagination. Whether you discuss them in a group or reflect on them personally, we hope they lead you to think more deeply and honestly about suffering and evil—and in the process connect with God in a more meaningful way.

1

If God Created Everything, Did He Create Evil?

Introduction

It was a Saturday night, and my wife and I (Chris) were arguing about the origin of evil. (Isn't that what *you* do on Saturday evenings?) We agreed the world is often a dark place, and the darkness had to start somewhere, sometime, with somebody.

"Adam and Eve," she said. "The Bible clearly says Adam and Eve gave into temptation and disobeyed God. Presto—sin and evil."

"I agree. But what role did God play in it?" I asked.

"None," she said confidently. "God is all good. Even more than that, he's love. And if God is love—one hundred percent, all the time—he can't create something that's not."

"I hear ya." I tried to keep this a conversation rather than an argument, yet I couldn't help myself. "But the Bible also portrays God as sovereign over everything, so he had to know that this was going to happen. Perhaps he was even in on it."

"Wait, what?" Now she was getting fired up. "Are you insinuating that God played a role in the creation of evil? I don't think so. It's not possible."

"I want to believe the same thing—and I'm stoked we're talking about it—but I'm just not as certain as you are," I said as I continued to think out loud.

Then I re-posed the question that ignited this passionate conversation in the first place: "If God is all-knowing and all-powerful, couldn't he create a world that was only good? And if he could—but he didn't—then is he not complicit in the making of evil?"

It's THE Question

For many people who do not believe in God (or the God of Christianity), the existence of evil and suffering is the reason. In Timothy Keller's stellar book *Walking with God through Pain and Suffering*, he restates the well-known argument.

> If you believe in a God who is all-powerful and sovereign over the world and at the same time is also perfectly good and just, then the existence of evil and suffering poses a problem. The classic statement of it was given by David Hume. . . . "Is he [God] willing to prevent evil but not able? Then he is impotent. Is he able but not willing? Then he is malevolent. Is he both able *and* willing? Whence then is evil?"[1]

Keller then comments, "Many insist that this problem is the single strongest objection to the existence of God in general and the plausibility of Christianity in particular."[2] In short, the existence of suffering and evil poses a major roadblock in the journey of faith for a lot of folks. In fact, this is probably the reason you picked up this book.

For eighteenth-century English philosopher David Hume—and much of humanity before and after him—these questions about God do more than wrinkle our brains. They rattle our feelings. We once heard Nicky Gumbel, a vicar in the Anglican Church, say, "Every intellectual objection to God has an emotional source."[3]

When ISIS warlords rape and murder innocents across the Middle East, we angrily question God's goodness. When divorce destroys a family, we wonder in sadness about his love. When a child goes unprotected, cancer goes uncured, and criminals go unstopped, we cry out, "Why?!" "Where are you?" "Why don't you do something?" Much of our wondering points to a profound inquiry: If God created everything, did he create evil?

This is a bold question. Those outside the church regularly raise objections to God based on the atrocities, injustice, and pain in life. But few of us in the body of Christ feel safe and free to courageously ask, is it all God's fault? If a trial was held and evidence given for the genesis of evil and suffering, would the final verdict declare God's guilt?

We must not be afraid. This is an important question to pose (that's putting it mildly!), as are each of the others in this book. Whether we admit it in public or not, many of us are wrestling with the toughest questions about suffering and evil. So let's get started.

QUESTIONS FOR REFLECTION AND DISCUSSION

- What is the reason you picked up this book?
- Has the existence of suffering and evil proved to be a roadblock in your belief in God? Why or why not?
- How have you wrestled with this issue before? How did you do it?
- How would you describe why suffering and evil exist?

God Created (Everything)

Aristotle, the ancient Greek philosopher, was the original teacher of cause and effect. He taught that everything had a cause, and each cause could be traced to its cause. But Aristotle argued that there was an original, primary cause that sparked it all. He called that primary cause the "unmoved mover."[4]

Christians can agree with Aristotle. The Bible teaches that it all started with one Supreme Being—God. Genesis 1:1 declares, "In the beginning God created the heavens and the earth." Bang. The Unmoved Mover set the universe in motion.

It doesn't stop with Genesis. Every corner of the Bible—the Psalms, Prophets, Gospels, and Epistles—describes God as the original initiator of all there is. Here's a snapshot:

> "You alone are the Lord. You made the skies and the heavens and all the stars. You made the earth and the seas and everything in them. You preserve them all, and the angels of heaven worship you."
>
> Nehemiah 9:6 NLT

> When I consider your heavens, the work of your fingers, the moon and the stars, which you have set in place, what is mankind that you are mindful of them, human beings that you care for them?
>
> Psalm 8:3–4

> In the beginning was the Word, and the Word was with God, and the Word was God. He was with God in the beginning. Through him all things were made; without him nothing was made that has been made.
>
> John 1:1–3

> The Son is the image of the invisible God, the firstborn over all creation. For in him all things were created: things in heaven and on earth, visible and invisible, whether thrones or powers or rulers or authorities; all things have been created through him and for him.
>
> Colossians 1:15–16

From beginning to end, the aggregate message of Scripture is that God made all we see and all we don't (see also Isaiah 42:5 and Revelation 4:11 for more). God made every human of every kind. He made hippopotamuses and the tiniest organisms still undiscovered. He made the sun that warms our summers and the stars no one has named. Everything that exists, according to the Bible, is God's doing.

That tees up our question nicely, then. If God made everything—the good and the bad, the gorgeous and the grotesque, the terrific and the terrible—does that include evil? Dare we ask? We must.

Is Evil a Thing?

I (Chris) recently saw a friend's old family photo in which his dad and uncle were proudly sporting Lilly Pulitzer pants. Not familiar with Pulitzer's style? Google her and you'll see how wild it is. It was the 1970s, and colorful patterned knickers were all the rage, apparently. I gawked at the men's crazy floral pants and wondered aloud, "Was that really a thing?" My friend answered, "Oh yeah, it was definitely a thing."

To say that evil is a "thing" in the way crazy pants are a thing would be flippant and foolish. Evil is no fad. It's never in vogue. So obviously, when we ask the question "Is evil a thing?" we mean, "Is it a created thing?" This question is pertinent because Christians believe God created everything. Every *thing*.

It is difficult philosophical work to try to describe what kind of thing evil is. But we do know this: Evil is not a run-of-the-mill object. You can't pick up a batch at the Evil Corner Market. You can't touch it, build it, transport it, or put it on your Amazon Wish List. Yet we all know evil is real. So are goodness, love, beauty, and dreams, but we can't grasp, construct, carry, or purchase them, either. With that in mind, we'll forgo the investigation into what kind of thing they are. The question instead is "Were they created?" We're not trying to split hairs to let God off the hook. We just want clarity. Stick with us as we think out loud.

It's clear that good and evil are not easily described or defined. In fact, if you substitute the words *good and evil* with *cactus and poodles*, answers will come much more easily. Cactus and poodles

17

can be seen, touched, and interacted with (we've got scars to prove it). And virtually anyone who graduated from kindergarten can describe both.

Evil, on the other hand, is not so easily wrangled. It is easy to include cactus and poodles in the list of "everything" God is responsible for, but it's more difficult with good and evil. Even so, we see the impact of good and evil in our world, our communities, and our lives. When we discuss good and evil together, we are even better able to set a definition and then, hopefully, get closer to discovering what role God played, if any, in the existence of evil.

Evil Is a Deprivation of Good

Like men and women, land and sea, and peanut butter and jelly, good and evil exist side by side yet are vastly different. In fact, one idea about the existence of evil states that evil simply cannot exist without good. This idea is called the deprivation of good. Evil, in other words, is the absence of good.

We have some friends who are architects and interior designers. They are fine artists who have introduced us to the concept of negative space. Imagine a completely empty room, with stark white walls. The room is full of space, but not negative space. Until, that is, you put a chair in the room. Now imagine taking one chair (a fancy new one or a janky old one, your call) and setting it against one of the blank, empty walls. Presto. The moment the chair is placed, negative space is created. Why? Because negative space is not the chair, but the now definable space around the chair. That space only exists because the chair exists.

Assuming we described the concept well, negative space helps us understand the deprivation of good. Deprivation is the lack or denial of something considered to be a necessity. We would all agree that good is an absolute necessity. No one survives without the good that God provides: love, joy, peace, hope, beauty, health, and relationships (to name only a few). Evil, then, occurs with the deprivation of good. The absence of good—the negative space around the existence of good—is the space in which evil exists, grows, and thrives.

In Frank Turek's book *Stealing from God*, he makes the same point that Saint Augustine did: "While evil is real, it's not a 'thing.' Evil doesn't exist on its own. It only exists as a lack or a deficiency in a good thing."[5] The argument is that evil can only exist if there is good, just as negative space around a chair can only exist if there is a chair. And there is little doubt that God created good.

But like good, evil does not exist in a vacuum. What is good can only be seen through the good that is done. Likewise, evil exists, but it is only experienced when someone does something evil. So the absence of good creates an opportunity for the presence of evil.

It's Also the Corruption of Good

An additional theory goes one step further. Some claim that evil is not simply the absence of good, but rather it is the corruption of good. Similarly then, evil is contingent on the preexistence of good.

In our society today, there is the proliferation of tragic and senseless school shootings, terror attacks, and acts of random violence. In the wake of these horrific and disgusting crimes, comments from the perpetrators' friends and families regularly reveal a strange phenomenon. Those close to the criminal will often say something to this effect: "We don't understand why he did this. He was a good person. He wouldn't hurt anyone."

These kinds of comments could stem from shock, and from the inability to see reality (i.e., anyone who murders innocent people is not a "good person," even if they are a close family member or friend), or the perpetrator was indeed good at one time. If the latter, then these comments lend to the belief that evil is the corruption of good.

In his book *The Goodness of God*, Randy Alcorn provides a succinct and thoughtful explanation.

> Evil cannot exist without the good it opposes. It's not so much the removal of good as it is the *corruption* of good. As metal does not need rust, but rust needs metal, so good doesn't need evil, but evil needs good. We can think of evil as a parasite on God's good creation. Without the living organism it uses as a host, the parasite cannot exist. Likewise, cancer thrives on, consumes, and ultimately kills healthy, living cells. Evil's corruption eats away at everything around it.[6]

Evil is a parasite that warps, twists, and ultimately destroys what is good. In its wake we see a trail of pain and suffering. Examples abound. Here are a few:

- *Knowledge*—God designed knowledge and wisdom as good gifts, but sin corrupts us, and we use knowledge to gain power, to advance at the expense of others, or to become our own "gods."
- *Relationships*—God invented human relationships, and he intended them for good. But when sex is used for manipulation and entertainment; marriages are disregarded when inconvenient; and friendships, partnerships, and family ties are exploited for power, greed, or self-advancement, God's design is contorted by evil into something harmful, destructive, objectifying, and painful.
- *Racial diversity*—God likes his diverse world. But we allow evil to eat away at what's good when our differences devolve into division, discord, and disrespect.
- *Natural resources*—All the earth was created good. But when sin runs rampant, the earth's bounty is consumed and

hoarded by the controlling few. We turn raw materials into harmful products and lay waste to land and ocean with no regard for the good life God has asked us to work and care for.

- *The church*—God's people are a good thing. But when evil creeps in, organized religion can be an incubator for greed, control, hate, and fear.

This list could go on and on. But the proof is in the pudding: Evil is more than only the absence of good; it is the corruption of good.

QUESTIONS FOR REFLECTION AND DISCUSSION

- Which of these two descriptions of evil—the absence of good and the corruption of good—makes the most sense to you? Can you think of another explanation for evil?
- How have you seen the presence of evil in the absence of good? How about in the corruption of something good?
- What leads to wrongdoing in your own life? How does your experience parallel with these ideas?

The Drift

Have you ever known of a couple who divorced and then remarried—to each other? Every once-dead-now-reborn marriage story is a miracle. Among those we've heard of, one stands out. The couple did not divorce because of infidelity, alcoholism, abuse, anger, or toxic in-laws. They split because of what they called "marriage drift." Their marriage dissolved because they simply stopped trying. They failed to intentionally cultivate what was good. Slowly, day by day, week by week, and month by month, they drifted apart. In the absence of effort, sacrifice, pursuit, and love, the subtle but disastrous force of distraction, selfishness, lack of concern, and pride took root. Without purposeful love and intentional growth, accidental indifference led to unintended destruction.

This is all too similar to what we see in the Bible. In fact, the first appearance of sin and evil happens, in part, because of a subtle but insidious drift.

The beginning of Genesis describes the origin of humanity in beautiful poetry. Grab your Bible and you'll see that God makes the heavens and earth, then caps this explosion of creativity with the invention of humanity, his favorite creatures. Genesis 1:27 tells us that "God created mankind in his own image, in the image of God he created them; male and female he created them." He places them in the perfect garden, giving them important work to do (see Genesis 2:15) along with precise instructions for thriving. When all is said and done, the Bible says, "Adam and his wife were both naked, and they felt no shame" (Genesis 2:25). This verse has nothing to do with physical nudity, and everything to do with the state of their souls.[7] They are whole. Complete. No fault or flaw, guilt or embarrassment. It was literally heaven on earth.

But then, in the very next chapter, something terrible happens. The serpent, armed with a handful of half-truths and a hatred for God, tries to turn their gaze from God to themselves. And it works. Adam and Eve disobey God, and their perfect world crashes in on them (see all of Genesis 3).

We cannot help but wonder (as you may be doing) what has happened between chapter 2 and chapter 3 of Genesis. At chapter 2's end, Adam and Eve stand tall, without shame, in the splendor of perfect relationship with God and one another. But early in chapter 3, Eve is all too willing to listen to a strange outsider, and she is no longer clear on God's original command. Close inspection reveals signs of "the drift."

In Genesis 3:1, the serpent subtly suggests that God said, "You must not eat from any tree in the garden." In truth, God said they must not eat of *one* tree in the garden (see Genesis 2:17). That's drift #1. Next, Eve adds her own slight change and claims God said, "You must not touch it, or you will die" (Genesis 3:3). But in Genesis 2:17 we see God said only that they must not *eat* of it. Drift #2.

The crafty serpent spots Eve's weakness and strikes. In a bald-faced lie, he tells Eve, "You will not certainly die" (Genesis 3:4). You can almost hear him scoff as he hints that Eve's Creator is wrong. She believes him. There's drift #3. And she eats.

This captivating dialogue reveals minor shifts with monumental results. We don't know how much time has elapsed after chapter 2, but by chapter 3 Eve no longer understands God's commands accurately. She stumbles over the serpent's suggestion and forgets God's explicit warning. She drifts from obedience to questioning, then questioning to disobedience. It's a drift from trust to doubt, then doubt to sin. And through the drift, evil corrupts what is good.

Now, before you accuse us (three male authors) of blaming the world's woes on one woman, let us quickly point out that Adam is adrift as well. Adam—the man God created to care for and protect his creation—is *silent*. His perfect, God-given companion, lover, and helper is tempted to throw away the keys of the kingdom, and he is passive, preoccupied, and pitiful. The devil has duped Eve, and Adam offers no resistance. "She also gave some [the forbidden fruit] to her husband, who was with her, and he ate it" (Genesis 3:6). Talk about drift! Adam, the man God imbued with purpose for perfect relationship (Genesis 2:19–25), has drifted into a lazy, disconnected, and sinful stupor.

This drift is bigger than any one individual. Adam drifted, Eve drifted, and sin and evil became a permanent thread in the fabric of the first family. Several millennia later, the world is full of pain and suffering because of humankind's continuous drift from God-honoring decisions to dishonorable ones. Instead of contributing to a flourishing world, we've fueled the world's demise.

Adam and Eve might have been the first, but they weren't the last. This drift appears in more than one passage of Scripture. The Old Testament history of the Jewish people is a roller-coaster ride. There are epic highs when they enjoy the privilege of worship, the fruit of obedience, and the blessing of God's favor. Then there are terrible lows, when God's people are exhibit A for rebellion, idolatry, and a lack of concern for God and others.

Isaiah's book describes their drift from beloved children to sinful rebels (see Isaiah 1). One psalmist described them as "a stubborn and rebellious generation, whose hearts were not loyal to God" (Psalm 78:8). God called the prophet Ezekiel to expose Israel's drift. God declared they "would not listen to me" and were not "careful to . . . follow my decrees" by which "the person who obeys them will live" (Ezekiel 20:8, 19, 21).

The drift continues in the New Testament. In Romans 1 Paul describes their epic slide into wickedness. "They exchanged the truth about God for a lie, and worshiped and served created things rather than the Creator" (Romans 1:25). Even a dynamic congregation—the church at Ephesus—forgot their first love and drifted from God. God, through the apostle John, told them, "You have forsaken the love you had at first. Consider how far you have fallen! Repent and do the things you did at first" (Revelation 2:4–5).

Sound familiar, Adam and Eve? Sound familiar, reader? It's embarrassingly familiar to us, that's for sure. We, the people of God, have often drifted from our first love, with evil as the result.

QUESTIONS FOR REFLECTION AND DISCUSSION

- Have you ever thought of sin in this way?
- Where have you seen signs of "the drift" in your life or the lives of others?
- How does this concept help (or hurt) your ideas on the origin of evil?

To Drift or Not to Drift, There Is No Question

In Matthew 12 Jesus spoke some powerfully unsettling words. He healed a demon-possessed man, and in irony of ironies, some religious leaders claimed this great display of God's power was actually the devil's work. Jesus responded to their foolishness with a statement that strikes at the core of the issue still today. He said,

"Whoever is not with me is against me, and whoever does not gather with me scatters" (verse 30).

The revelation is this: There is no such thing as neutral ground. Jesus said that if we do not intentionally trust God, move toward God, and act for God, then we are distrusting him, moving away from him, and acting against him.

People mistakenly believe there is a spiritual Switzerland. We think we can take no sides, keep still and quiet, and avoid contributing to the evil by ignoring it. God says otherwise. It's difficult to hear, but deep down we know it's true. Real life is caught in a cosmic battle. There is good. There is evil. And there is no in-between. Our reticence (or even laziness) to acknowledge, thank, obey, and pursue God does not leave us in neutral territory. Like floating in a river, one is never still.

Like Adam and Eve, our selfward focus and deep-seated belief that we know better than God (even if we don't admit it out loud) carry us further away from what is good. As we drift, we give evil the negative space it needs to corrupt what God created as good.

An important final question could be this: If there is no neutral ground between good and evil, why didn't God throw us a bone and just eliminate evil? No evil, no options. No options, no drift. No drift, no evil! Right? It's a great question, and it gets to the heart of God's love for us.

Good and Evil = Love

What if we suggested that the existence of evil is proof of God's love? Before you respond by setting fire to this little book, please read this section. We think it's important, and we think you will agree.

Alvin Plantinga is a follower of Jesus who is also one of the most influential American philosophers of the twentieth century. Plantinga faithfully taught and wrote about philosophy in premier universities for sixty years. He's one smart cookie.

Plantinga's "free-will defense" is his well-known philosophical explanation for how the existence of evil does not disprove the existence of a good God. It's readily accepted by most important thinkers, Christian and non-Christian alike. Plantinga wrote,

> A world containing creatures who are significantly free (and freely perform more good than evil actions) is more valuable, all else being equal, than a world containing no free creatures at all. Now God can create free creatures, but He can't cause or determine them to do only what is right. For if He does so, then they aren't significantly free after all; they do not do what is right freely. To create creatures capable of moral good, therefore, He must create creatures capable of moral evil.[8]

That's a mind-full. But Plantinga's philosophy is vital for understanding good, evil, and God's love. In short and simple terms, true love is contingent on choice. If there's no choice, there's no freedom, and if there's no freedom, there's no love. If God created humans only capable of good, we would be robots (good little robots, but still robots). Slavery is never loving, even if the slave is required to do good. God loves us so much that he grants us the freedom to choose something other than him.

Another brilliant Christian thinker, C. S. Lewis, wrote, "Christianity asserts that God is good; that he made all things good and for the sake of their goodness; that one of the good things He made, namely, the free will of rational creatures, by its very nature included the possibility of evil."[9] In this view, God did not create evil. Rather, the very nature of love makes evil a possibility.

The Deep End

Can we acknowledge something helpful? We are in the deep end of the pool here. Wrestling with questions like "If God created everything, did he create evil?" is no easy task. These are *big* questions—the toughest questions. It's difficult to land on a simple, easy answer, and more often than not, life is not tied up in neat little bows.

What we see in Scripture and life is that evil exists. It exists in the absence of good, as the corruption of good, and because life without the possibility of something not good is not actually good.

God, out of his love for us, gives us the freedom to reject him. And unfortunately for us and our world, we have chosen that route far too often for much too long. Alvin Plantinga, in the continuation of his earlier cited words, writes it well:

> As it turned out, sadly enough, some of the free creatures God created went wrong in the exercise of their freedom; this is the source of moral evil. The fact that free creatures sometimes go wrong, however, counts neither against God's omnipotence nor against His goodness; for He could have forestalled the occurrence of moral evil only by removing the possibility of moral good.[10]

We will further unpack this idea as you read on, so keep turning pages. We will also see that God—the One who never ignores evil and dared to enter the evil to save us from it—offers hope as nothing, and no one, else can. Evil may exist, but there is a good God who has—and will—defeat evil and remedy suffering.

In the meantime, these questions are good ones. Let's keep asking them. . . .

QUESTIONS FOR REFLECTION AND DISCUSSION

- Have you ever encountered ideas about suffering and evil before? If so, when and where?
- What is your response to the idea that love necessitates evil?
- Are you comfortable with mystery? Does the idea of not fully understanding God's ways bother you? Why or why not?
- How might the existence of evil fall into the category of mystery?

2

Why Is There Suffering and Evil in a World Made Good by God?

Introduction

Imagine one of Christianity's most influential thinkers, whose books have convinced millions to consider the claims of Jesus Christ, coming to a point in his life where he doubted the goodness of God. That's exactly what happened to C. S. Lewis, arguably the most quoted Christian writer this side of the apostle Paul. It wasn't a crisis of faith, where something he believed was no longer true. It was a crisis of grief, where someone he loved was taken from him. Does that surprise you? It shouldn't, because Lewis's experience isn't all that different from that of many Christians. It could be your experience.

Lewis's most famous book is *Mere Christianity*, where he builds a brilliant apologetic for the existence and trustworthiness of God. But it's in his last book, *A Grief Observed*, first published in 1961 under the pseudonym N. W. Clerk and then republished in his own name after his death in 1963, where Lewis is most honest and direct concerning his view of God. Written after the passing of Joy Davidman, his wife of just four years, the book is short, real, and raw.

His arguments in *Mere Christianity* about the existence of God and the truth of the Christian faith are logical and convincing. But for emotional power, they can't match the depth of his anguish in *A Grief Observed* as Lewis comes to terms with his anger and confusion about the God he believed in.

Early in the book, Lewis states something we have all experienced. When you are happy, you have no sense of needing God. In this state, you feel you could ask anything and be "welcomed with open arms." But when you are in trouble, when you are desperate, what do you find when you reach out to God? "A door slammed in your face, and a sound of bolting and double bolting on the inside. After that, silence."[1]

Lewis asks what this means, and he answers with a question: "Why is He so present a commander in our time of prosperity and so very absent a help in our time of trouble?"[2]

Let's Start with the Bad News

The Christian faith is filled with paradoxes: The weak become strong, the wise are made foolish, the last shall be first, and the way to save your life is to lose it. Here's another paradox to ponder: For some reason there is suffering and evil in a world that was made good by God. Even more puzzling, bad stuff exists right under the nose of a God who is good.

As we said in the last chapter, the question of the goodness of God weighed against the evil and suffering in the world is *the* question about God that most troubles people. At the very least, the question—if left unanswered—poses a major roadblock in the journey of faith for a lot of people. So we can't sweep it under the rug. We have to deal with it. In her stark and sometimes shocking book on the subject, Annie Dillard puts it this way: "For the world is as glorious as ever, and exalting, but for credibility's sake, let's start with the bad news."[3]

The bad news is all around us. Oh, we try to be philosophical and think that the bad stuff that happened in the past—child sacrifices, gas chambers, cannibalism, slavery—is worse than the stuff that happens now, but we're only kidding ourselves. The wars, atrocities, mayhem, diseases, and natural disasters are every bit as intense now as they have been in the past. If anything, things are worse, because there are more people doing really bad things to more people, which means there are more people being affected by evil and suffering.

Day in and day out, we see terrible things, not necessarily with our own eyes, but through the eyes of others. It used to be that the stories of suffering and evil came to us in the morning newspapers and the evening news. With the development of the smartphone, however, the news comes in a constant stream. If you were so inclined, you could find examples of suffering and evil throughout the day (we don't recommend this) because it's right there in your pocket.

It's possible to ignore the stream of bad news, or even become desensitized to it, but the effects remain. At the end of the day, we need someone to blame. And since nobody on earth seems capable of solving the big problems in our world, we have to set our sights higher. And there sits God, an easy target for a simple question: If God is so good, why are things so bad? Or to put it in the form of a statement rather than a question, we might conclude, "Because there is so much suffering and evil in the world, God mustn't be all that good."

This is exactly the conclusion C. S. Lewis came to as he wrestled with the death of his wife. The pain he was experiencing didn't cause him to stop believing in God. It actually did something much worse. "The conclusion I dread is not 'So there's no God after all,' but 'So this is what God's really like. Deceive yourself no longer.'"[4] Later in the book, Lewis poses the question that is at the heart of this chapter. "What reason have we, except our own desperate wishes, to believe that God is, by any standard we can conceive, 'good'? Doesn't all the *prima facie* evidence suggest exactly the opposite?"[5]

Disappointment with God

We suspect that Lewis's conclusion represents the feeling many Christians have when bad things happen. We don't stop believing in God. Instead we get disappointed with him. That's the theme and the title of Philip Yancey's classic book *Disappointment with God*. Yancey believes that when we go to God for help in our distress, and we feel he has slammed the door in our face, we often come to one or more of three conclusions:

- God is unfair.
- God is silent.
- God is hidden.

Let's turn these statements into questions and see what happens.

Is God Unfair?

Fairness is something we all want in every circumstance. From the time we are young we want to be treated fairly. "Billy's cookie is bigger than mine! That's not fair!" As we grow older, we never get over the feeling of being slighted, especially when the stakes get higher. So when something much more serious than disproportionate cookie size is at stake, we raise the stakes in our complaining. And when something terrible happens that is beyond our ability to solve, and we can't imagine anyone else solving it, we have no one to blame but God.

As an approach to this question, Yancey uses the example of God's people—otherwise known as the Israelites—in the Old Testament. God established a series of laws to guide their behavior. If they obeyed, things would go well for them. They would receive protection from their enemies and other stresses that plague humanity. On the other hand, if they disobeyed God's laws, they would suffer at the hands of the surrounding nations, if not the hand of God himself.[6]

When you read the Old Testament, you see a cycle of obedience and disobedience, of the Israelites following God and being blessed, and then forgetting about him and being punished, only to cry out that God is being unfair. Here's a passage from the book of Judges that shows this cycle in the span of just two verses:

> Whenever the Lord raised up a judge for them, he was with the judge and saved them out of the hands of their enemies as long as the judge lived; for the Lord relented because of their groaning under those who oppressed and afflicted them. But when the judge died, the people returned to ways even more corrupt than those of their ancestors, following other gods and serving and worshiping them. They refused to give up their evil practices and stubborn ways. Therefore the Lord was very angry with Israel.
>
> Judges 2:18–20

It's frustrating to read about these cycles. Don't these people see what's going on? Why won't they learn from their mistakes?

But then we have to look at ourselves and wonder if we're all that different. Do we not ignore God when things are going well and cry out to him when we're in the proverbial toilet? We can read about the disobedience of people in the Bible and say with no small amount of pride, "At least we aren't like those Israelites." In fact, we can look at any period in history, or any one of many situations in our world today, and say, "Sure glad we're not as bad as they are."

Truth is, we are as bad. We are just as filled with evil thoughts and spiritual rebellion, even if we don't always act on them. Maybe we haven't tortured anyone or sacrificed a child to Molek, but what we view as mildly offensive behavior, God sees as wretchedness. Is it any wonder that God seems distant when we cry out to him only when we're in a jam? We're disappointed in God? How do you think he feels about us?

Thankfully, the story of the Bible doesn't stop with the Old Testament and God's law. We have the New Testament and the demonstration of God's love in the form of Jesus Christ. The apostle Paul, once a persecutor of Christians in the first century, puts it this way:

> Very rarely will anyone die for a righteous person, though for a good person someone might possibly dare to die. But God demonstrates his own love for us in this: While we were still sinners, Christ died for us.
>
> Romans 5:7–8

As Yancey points out, the Old Testament (or Old Covenant) was about keeping agreements we are incapable of fulfilling—not because we don't want to, but because we can't.[7] By comparison, the New Testament (or New Covenant) is based on God's grace and God's forgiveness. "He saved us, not because of righteous things we had done, but because of his mercy" (Titus 3:5). It doesn't matter who we are or what we have done or what we've been through. God is willing, ready, and able to forgive us. That's not just fairness. It's unconditional love and incredible grace.

QUESTIONS FOR REFLECTION AND DISCUSSION

- What is it about humans that causes us to get into these cycles where we obey and disobey God?
- The passage in Judges says the Lord relented because of the groaning of his people, and then became angry when they

> returned to their evil ways. Is God any different in the way he treats us today?
> • Are all sins equal in the eyes of God? Why or why not?

Is God Silent?

We may accept that God is fair, but what about those times when God is silent? We've experienced this ourselves. So have you. And it's not that God is silent only when you are desperate. Sometimes you call out from a heart that is affectionate toward God and a life that is trying to please him, and you don't feel all that close to him. Sometimes you ask for wisdom, seeking God's will for a big decision, and all you get are crickets. How does that make you feel? Here's how one of the writers in the book of Psalms expresses it:

> O God, do not remain silent; do not turn a deaf ear, do not stand aloof, O God.
>
> Psalm 83:1

We know a longtime Christian whose grandchild died in a freak accident. We attended the memorial service and the reception that followed, where we offered our condolences. With tears in his eyes, our friend looked at us and said, "How could this have been God's will? I just can't accept that." We didn't respond. We were just *there*. What can you say at a moment like this? There is nothing we can say, because we don't know the answer. We don't know why God is silent. It's so very frustrating.

Yet we know enough about God to eliminate two possible reasons for his silence. First, God isn't silent because he can't hear us. "The Lord hears the needy," declares the psalmist David (Psalm 69:33). The book of Proverbs tells us, "The Lord is far from the wicked, but he hears the prayer of the righteous" (Proverbs 15:29). John the apostle writes, "This is the confidence we have in approaching God: that if we ask anything according to his will, he hears us" (1 John 5:14).

35

Second, God isn't silent because he is ignoring us. He may be working "behind the scenes" for our benefit in ways we do not yet understand. When we don't even know how to pray, God is helping us. "In the same way, the Spirit helps us in our weakness," Paul writes. "We do not know what we ought to pray for, but the Spirit himself intercedes for us through wordless groans" (Romans 8:26).

Yancey again uses the Israelites as our example. There were plenty of times when God was very vocal and specific about what he wanted his people to do, and it was always for their own good. In fact, God was quite chatty about it. For example, shortly after God rescued the Israelites from their Egyptian oppressors, they started grumbling about their lack of food. "If only we had died by the Lord's hand in Egypt!" they complained to their leaders, Moses and Aaron. "There we sat around pots of meat and ate all the food we wanted, but you have brought us out into this desert to starve this entire assembly to death" (Exodus 16:3).

God didn't like the grumbling, but he understood their need, so he provided food in the form of "manna," which quite literally came from heaven. God then explained very carefully how they were to collect and eat it. Of course, you know enough of the story by now to know what happened. Some followed God's instructions, but others ignored it. Yancey observes,

> The very clarity of God's will had a stunting effect on the Israelites' faith. Why pursue God when he had already revealed himself so clearly? Why step out in faith when God had already guaranteed the results? Why wrestle with the dilemma of conflicting choices when God had already solved the dilemma?[8]

We see time and time again that God's clear and active guidance does not necessarily lead to better faith. If anything, writes Yancey, "clear guidance sucks away freedom, making every choice a matter of obedience rather than faith."[9]

Maybe you're hurting right now, like our friend who is grieving the loss of his grandchild. Have you been praying, asking God for help, for answers, for anything at all, and all you hear is silence? Perhaps God is asking you to trust him in the dark. If your path was well-illuminated and you could see everything, would you need God to guide you? Would you need God at all? If you knew why you are in distress, would you be content? Like our friend, you may have good reasons for rejecting the idea that your troubles are part of God's will. But just because God isn't answering you right now doesn't mean he doesn't care. Just because he's silent doesn't mean he isn't there.

QUESTIONS FOR REFLECTION AND DISCUSSION

- How do you feel when you cry out to God and he is silent?
- What are the benefits of God's silence in your life?
- Describe an experience when you discovered after the fact that God was working behind the scenes.

Is God Hidden?

The question about the hiddenness of God may be asked another way: "Why doesn't God make himself more obvious?" That's the question we pose in our book *Answering the Toughest Questions About God and the Bible*. As Yancey does, we go to the Old Testament and consider just how obvious God can be:

- He sent a series of plagues on Egypt that convinced Pharaoh to release his Hebrew slaves, yet Pharaoh didn't believe (Exodus 4:4–9; 5:2).
- A generation of Israelites witnessed miracle after miracle, yet they constantly refused to follow God fully (Numbers 14:26–38).[10]

In the New Testament, we have Jesus, who is the visible image of the invisible God, performing miracles, healing diseases, even raising the dead to life, yet many chose not to believe.

And what about us? We don't necessarily see the kinds of miracles we read about in the Bible, but we still see miraculous things. Even more convincingly, we experience God's presence in our lives, often in our darkest, most desperate moments. We may say we want physical proof that God is there, but would that help? It didn't help Pharaoh or the Pharisees. As Yancey observes, just as God's vocal interaction with his people didn't promote belief, "God's visible presence did nothing to improve lasting faith."[11]

In another one of those Christian paradoxes we talked about earlier, it's the suffering itself that has the power to drive us to greater faith. As Lewis continued in his personal journey of grief at the end of his life, he came to understand how this works: It's in the struggle that we begin to see God for who he truly is. C. S. Lewis uses the illustration of a rope to demonstrate. "You never know how much you really believe anything until its truth or falsehood becomes a matter of life and death to you," he writes. "It's easy to believe a rope is strong and sound as long as you are merely using it to cord a box. But suppose you had to hang by that rope over a precipice. Wouldn't you then discover how much you really trusted it?"[12]

Until the stakes are really high, we tend to treat God as a kind of accessory, someone to believe but not really trust. Lewis continues: "Nothing less will shake a man—or at any rate a man like me—out of his merely verbal thinking and his merely notional beliefs. He has to be knocked silly before he comes to his senses. Only torture will bring out the truth. Only under torture does he discover it himself."[13]

What Doesn't Kill Us Makes Us Stronger

Even those with no stated belief in God understand the value of evil and suffering. Friedrich Nietzsche's famous quote "What doesn't kill us makes us stronger" is a constant refrain in literature and music. And here's the thing: As soon as we read or hear the phrase, we know what it means. We can identify.

For the Christian, coming to realize this concept through personal experience brings us closer to understanding how God works through our pain. When things are going well, we hold God at arm's length. When we're going through a struggle, we run to God like a drowning person reaches for a lifeline. As we cling to him, desperate for an answer and perhaps even salvation, we begin to realize that the rope he offers is strong enough to hold us. And when we get through the pain and suffering we are experiencing, we become stronger in the struggle.

There's a flip side to all of this. When we experience loss, when we are going through a dark time, our immediate tendency is to question the goodness of God. But as we come to grips with how often we disappoint God rather than the other way around, it's a wonder things go well for us at all. Timothy Keller echoes Yancey when he writes,

> When we stand back to consider the premise—that God owes us a good life—it is clearly unwarranted. If there really is an infinite glorious God, why should the universe revolve around us rather than around him? If we look at the biblical God's standards for our behavior—the Golden Rule, the Ten Commandments, and the Sermon on the Mount—and then consider humanity's record against those norms, it may occur to us that the real riddle of evil is not what we thought. Perhaps the real puzzle is this: Why, in light of our behavior as a human race, does God allow so much *happiness?*[14]

QUESTIONS FOR REFLECTION AND DISCUSSION

- Why doesn't physical proof of God lead people to believe in him?
- Reflect on this statement: "It's in the struggle that we begin to see God for who he truly is." Who is God to you in your struggles?
- In what ways have you disappointed God? Do you think it matters to him? In what way?

When We Don't Know Why

In this chapter we have been considering a basic question that all religions must answer: "Why is there suffering and evil in a world made good by God?" While other belief systems either (a) expect you to work harder in order to overcome, or (b) deny that evil is a problem, Christianity alone acknowledges the reality of evil and offers a solution. It's a solution based on trusting God even when we don't know why. And how do we know we can trust him when we're going through a trial and all the evidence seems to point to a God who has abandoned us and doesn't seem good at all? We suggest three reasons.

First, we have the historical records (that would be the Bible). Reading about God's provision for Israel in their darkest hours should give us some kind of assurance. These aren't stories written for our enjoyment. They are for our benefit so that we can learn how God interacts with us.

Second, we have our own experiences with God. How often have we gotten into trouble, been the victims of an injustice, or watched as a loved one suffered, with no clue as to how God is working, only to emerge on the other side with a clearer understanding? In his essay "When We Don't Know Why, We Trust God Who Knows Why," Os Guinness approaches it this way: "Christians do not say, 'I do not understand you at all, but I trust you anyway.' Rather we say, 'I do not understand you *in this situation*, but I *understand why I trust you anyway*. Therefore I can trust that you understand even though I don't.'"[15]

Third, we have Jesus Christ, the ultimate expression of God's love and goodness. "For Christians, the answer to the question, 'How may I be sure that God is there and that God is good?' is answered satisfactorily only in Jesus Christ. Any 'proof' of God's existence or argument in favor of his goodness that ends elsewhere is bound to be inconclusive or wrong."[16]

If you are an active follower of Jesus, you already know this and have no doubt experienced his presence personally. Still, it's not easy, and tougher still for those whose belief in God is still in process. If that's the case with you, all we would ask is that you consider how God may be working in your life right now. The Bible says—and we believe—that God is working everything for your good as you love him (see Romans 8:28–30). Things in your life may not be going the way you would like, and you may feel that God is anything but good. But you can be sure, even if you don't know why, that God is not withholding anything good from you, because he has given you his Son. There's no greater good that God could have given you.

The Hardest Peace

One of the most beautiful stories we've read in recent years is told by Kara Tippetts in her book *The Hardest Peace*. Kara's life was turned upside down with the discovery that cancer was ravaging her body. Kara and her husband, a pastor, and their children had moved to a new town to take on a new church when she discovered the "crushing reality" of her diagnosis. Kara's perspective is gripping and instructive.

> I was met with an unexpected disease—unexpected in every way. I could never have dreamed the endless appointments sitting on the crinkled paper of doctors' tables and the endless treatment to extend my days. I never expected to be planning my funeral, counting my moments, and fighting for my next breath in my thirties. I never expected to be sitting on my daughter's bed with the sinking feeling her mama was going to die of cancer and not of old age, and not knowing the right words to love her well. Never. But those places, those raw, broken places, are the heart of life. The brokenness of today causes us to look to tomorrow and hope for it. It causes us to ask, "What is it all for?" I could not look with confidence into the face of my young daughter Harper Joy and tell her I would be with her into my old age—that simply doesn't look like my story. No, but I could confidently begin to tell her about heaven.

Behold, I am making all things new.

Revelation 21:5[17]

QUESTIONS FOR REFLECTION AND DISCUSSION

- What difference does it make that Christianity alone acknowledges the reality of evil and offers a solution? Is this important to you? Why or why not?

- In what way is Jesus the answer to the question "How may I be sure that God is there and that God is good?"

3

Why Doesn't God Eliminate Suffering and Evil?

Introduction

"I used to be a Christian." The young woman sitting next to me (Stan) on a cross-country flight made the statement with no emotion. We had just exchanged answers to the "What do you do for a living?" question. "I'm a medical technician," she said. I told her I was involved in Christian publishing. The way she responded to my profession startled me somewhat, though I tried not to show it. Fortunately, she had her eyes on a copy of a book resting on her lap. It was *The God Delusion* by renowned atheist Richard Dawkins.

Undeterred by neither her declaration nor her book, I followed up with the only question I could think of. "What happened?" I asked. "What happened that caused you to leave your Christian faith?" She answered with just one word: "Orlando." I played the odds and eliminated Disney World as the cause of her journey from belief to unbelief (although I have heard stories of parents who were ready to punch Mickey Mouse in the face after braving excessive heat and oppressive lines at the Magic Kingdom . . . but I digress). Pressing for clarity, I asked, "Why Orlando?"

"It was the shooting in the gay nightclub in Orlando that left one hundred people dead or injured," she replied. "I used to believe in God, that he was good and powerful. But Orlando changed things for me. I decided right then that I couldn't believe in a God that would allow that to happen."

The Question of God and Evil

We've already established that the question about God and evil is *the* question. It troubles people of all ages, of all backgrounds, at any point in their journey of faith. And if the girl on the plane is any kind of example for us, we have to deal with the power this question has to undermine or even shatter belief in God. From our experience, it isn't so much that evil exists that troubles people most. It's that God doesn't seem all that interested in doing away with it.

Furthermore, it isn't evil itself that is a problem for people. It's the effect that evil has. Seeing people mowed down in a nightclub. Reading about young girls kidnapped in Africa by terrorists. Seeing images of people in desperately poor countries suffer as a result of natural disasters. It's the sum total of human misery that bothers us. Human suffering gives evil a face and a personality, and without answers, that face and that personality become synonymous with God.

The problem of evil is distinct from the problem of suffering in that suffering is the byproduct of evil. Suffering wouldn't be a reality in our lives and in the world if evil did not exist. In chapter 1 we posited that evil is not a "thing" in itself, like cactus or poodles, but rather the deprivation and the corruption of good. In other words, evil exists because good exists. "Evil is a parasite," we said, "that warps, twists, and ultimately destroys what is good." Makes sense, right? But does this help us answer the question posed by

44

this chapter? "Why does God allow evil?" Or more to the point: "Why doesn't God get rid of evil?"

QUESTIONS FOR REFLECTION AND DISCUSSION

- How would you have responded to the girl on the plane?
- Have you ever been close to giving up on God because of something terrible that happened in the world or to you personally? What happened?

Three Perspectives on God and Evil

It's not an easy question to answer, so we're going to start by talking about *approaches* rather than *answers*. You will see some classic arguments that we hope will begin to address the concerns you may have, whether you believe in God, struggle to believe, or don't believe at all. These answers will not be satisfying—intellectual responses rarely are—but we hope they inform your thinking as you work through this problem.

Our approaches to evil are based on three different perspectives:

- *If you believe in God*, you probably take the question about God and evil very personally. You've experienced the love and goodness of God, so the shattering effects of evil can potentially shake your belief in a good and loving God. It's important for you to wrestle with this question, especially if you have been the victim of something evil. If you don't formulate a satisfying response, your faith could be damaged or (in the case of the girl on the plane) shattered.
- *If you are skeptical about God*, you may have already concluded that the strongest argument against his existence is the ongoing and unabated presence of evil in the world. You likely would agree with the girl on the plane—that certain acts of evil are enough to abandon your belief in God—although

you stop short of declaring with absolute certainty that he doesn't exist.

- *If you don't believe God exists*, you have concluded that the existence of evil proves the God of Scripture doesn't exist because it's logically impossible.

Why Doesn't God Stop Evil?

In our book *Evidence for Faith 101*, we present the classic argument for why God and evil are incompatible, often presented by skeptics and those who don't believe in God based on the reality of evil.

1. An all-powerful God would be able to eliminate evil.
2. An all-good God would want to eliminate evil.
3. But evil exists.[1]

The idea behind the argument is that all these claims must be held by the Christian, and if that's the case, say skeptics and atheists, then you must logically come to one of two conclusions. Because evil exists . . .

- . . . *God is neither all-powerful nor all-good*. This is the conclusion favored by skeptics, who aren't ready to declare God nonexistent, but they abandon their faith in him because they are so troubled by suffering and evil and God's apparent unwillingness to do anything about them (like the girl on the plane).
- . . . *the God of Christianity does not exist*. This is the conclusion favored by atheists. Because the God of Christianity is both unwilling and unable to stop evil, such a God must not exist. Of course, when you take God out of the picture, you still have to account for the existence of evil, which presents a challenge for the atheist (we will discuss this a little later).

46

A Reasonable Response

Skeptics and atheists say Christians must agree with all three statements in their argument. Let's look at the first two statements and see if that's the case.

An all-powerful God would be able to eliminate evil. This statement presupposes that God can do anything, but isn't this a false presupposition? Are there not some things God can't do? If God is holy, can he lie? Because he is perfect, can he make a mistake? Because he is eternal, can God cease to exist? We believe the answer to questions like these is no. There are certain things God can't do. With that in mind, consider something else God can't do. It relates directly to the reality of evil: *God cannot make free moral agents who can never go wrong.*

Remember our mention of Alvin Plantinga's "free-will defense" in chapter 1? There is a logical sequence in that argument that may surprise you:

1. A world with moral good is better than a world with no moral good.
2. Only free agents can do moral good.
3. Even God cannot create free moral agents who can never go wrong.

The effect of this argument, which is widely accepted by professional philosophers, is to conclude that it is possible for God and evil to exist without diminishing God's character or abilities. In their book *Is God Just a Human Invention?*, Sean McDowell and Jonathan Morrow make this observation about the free-will defense: "Implicit in Plantinga's argument is that God did not create evil and is not implicated in the evil humans actualized when they misused their freedom."[2]

An all-good God would want to eliminate evil. This statement presupposes that God is only good when he eliminates evil. But this is an incomplete picture of God's goodness, which includes

God's creation of free moral agents, who have the freedom to do wrong along with the freedom to do good. The philosopher Peter Kreeft, when asked, "Why didn't God create a world without human freedom?", explains it this way:

> Because that would have been a world without humans. Would it have been a place without suffering? Yes. But it also would have been a world without love, which is the highest value in the universe. That highest good never could have been experienced. Real love—our love of God and our love of each other—must involve a choice. But with the granting of that choice comes the possibility that people would choose instead to hate.[3]

QUESTIONS FOR REFLECTION AND DISCUSSION

- Of the three perspectives on God and evil, which one most closely reflects the view of American culture?
- Had it ever occurred to you that God cannot make free moral agents who can never go wrong? How does this change your perspective on God and evil?
- How can God be good and yet allow evil?

Less Than Satisfied?

You may have to review the preceding pages a few times for the force and logic of the arguments to sink in. We had to review them several times! After you've wrestled with these intellectual arguments, you may find yourself agreeing with Plantinga and other smart people that God is technically off the hook when it comes to the existence of evil. However, it may not be enough to know in your head that the presence of evil doesn't discount or eliminate the existence of an all-good and all-powerful God.

When you've taken some time to wrestle with these intellectual arguments, we suspect that the conclusions won't be all that satisfying even if you believe those conclusions to be true. We can say all we want that *people* are the cause of evil—it was the shooter and not God who killed those people in Orlando—but we still end up holding God responsible. Why is that?

Tim Keller proposes that "most people who, in the face of actual evil, object to God's existence do so not for philosophical reasons but for visceral ones."[4] Whether it's the girl on the plane or someone you know, people respond to the problem of evil from the heart rather than from the mind. They may believe in their head that evil doesn't disprove the existence of God, or that humans are the cause of most of the evil in the world, but they cannot emotionally accept a God who would allow such evil.

Maybe that's where you are. If so, we can sympathize. The reminders of evil are all around us, invading our senses and disrupting our happy thoughts. The Orlando shooting is just one example. Atrocities are commonplace in our world, and every time something horrible happens, we look for answers, usually revolving around the question "Why, God?" Even the most committed Christian has to admit that there seem to be no clear reasons why God doesn't do something about evil. As a result, we may not agree with the atheist who believes that evil disproves God's existence, but we have sympathy for those who hesitate to trust a God who would let these things happen.

We're Not the First Ones

You might think we are the first ones to find the topic of God and evil distressing. In fact, people have been frustrated about this very thing for quite a long time. See if you can't identify with this plea:

> How long, Lord, must I call for help, but you do not listen? Or cry out to you, "Violence!" but you do not save? Why do you make me look at injustice? Why do you tolerate wrongdoing? Destruction and violence are before me; there is strife, and conflict abounds.
>
> Habakkuk 1:2–3

These words could have been written in a blog post last week by someone in one of America's strife-torn cities. Or in a letter written from Europe during World War II. Or by a soldier in the Civil War. All would have provided appropriate settings. But this passage wasn't written by a soldier or a civilian. It was written 2,600 years ago by one of God's prophets, Habakkuk.

Habakkuk is known as a minor prophet, not because his writings are less important than a "major" prophet like Isaiah, but because his book is shorter. The occasion of Habakkuk's book was the period of time between the fall of Nineveh in 612 BC and the destruction of Jerusalem in 586 BC at the hands of the Babylonians. God sent Habakkuk to the people of Judah, who were enjoying prosperity in a nation filled with violence and wickedness. They were ignoring God even though their nation had been founded on God's law.

At the beginning of his short book, Habakkuk asks God the "why" question about evil in a way that echoes our own concerns:

- How long must I call for help?
- Why do you make me look at injustice?
- Why do you tolerate wrongdoing?

Because he is a prophet of God, Habakkuk gets to hear from God directly. In fact, his book is a dialogue between the prophet and God. Thankfully for us, Habakkuk writes down what God says so we can also hear the words of God.

Isn't it amazing how the Bible works? From God's mouth to the prophet's pen to our ears (see 2 Peter 1:21). When we read the Word of God, we can be confident God is speaking to us and all who believe him. So what exactly did God tell Habakkuk? Basically, God declares that he uses evil to accomplish his purposes. In other words, he uses it for good. Here's how Wilson Benton explains it:

> God says, "Habakkuk, you want to know how I, as a holy God, can use evil to accomplish good. . . . You don't know what I'm doing,

but Habakkuk, you can believe that *I know* what I'm doing. Even though you don't understand how good can come of this, you can believe that I understand how I am using all of this for your good."[5]

Like all of us, Habakkuk wanted answers. He wanted to know why God was allowing evil. He wanted to understand everything. As God answered him, the prophet realized that God's purposes far outweighed his ability to understand. Using evil to accomplish good? How can that be? In his answer to Habakkuk's questions, God responded with words that are the bedrock of the good news story of God: "The righteous shall live by his faith" (Habakkuk 2:4 ESV). Habakkuk didn't know how God was going to save his people and make things right, but God didn't need his understanding. God needed his trust.

QUESTIONS FOR REFLECTION AND DISCUSSION

- Why is the problem of evil more visceral than intellectual?
- What does it say about God that one of his own prophets can question God the way he does and not get into trouble?
- Why does God need your trust but not your understanding?

Good Coming Out of the Pain

We want you to pause for a moment and think about something tragic that's happened in our world. What was the result? While you're thinking, allow us to tell you about something we experienced.

Recently we visited the 9/11 Memorial and Museum in New York City. The memorial comprises the two large spaces dug into the same footprint as the twin towers of the World Trade Center. Around the perimeters of each one-acre space are the names of the 2,983 victims of the horrific act of terror that occurred on September 11, 2001.

The museum is a stunning and sobering experience that is also below ground. As you tour the museum, you descend to the foundation level of the twin towers. All around are sights and sounds of that fateful morning that envelop visitors as they walk through the museum. The experience is profoundly moving, but it is also eerily inspiring. Even though you are in a vast subterranean cavern, your spirits are somehow lifted as you watch, read, and listen to the dramatic stories of heroism that occurred in the aftermath of the attacks.

America was rocked to its core on that day, but in the aftermath, as difficult as the journey was—and it is still a difficult process for many people—the light of hope and even the effect of God's grace were evident. In a very real sense, as you leave the museum, ascending to ground level once again, you have the distinct impression that it was faith that brought us this far, and it is faith that will get us through.

Like us, you can probably think of a similar experience, whether it happened to a nation, a city, or a family. It was no doubt horrible and anguishing. But as deep and enduring as the pain has been, can you think of something good that came out of it? How has your own faith been affected by that event or those particular circumstances? *"Even though you don't understand how good can come of this, you can believe that I understand how I am using all of this for your good. The just shall live by faith."*[6]

The Greatest Tragedy Is Our Greatest Hope

Wilson Benton asks several questions that are central to this whole business of God and evil: "What's the greatest tragedy this world has ever seen? What is the worst crime that has ever been committed? What is the most horrible thing that has every happened in the history of mankind?"[7] His answer to all three questions? The crucifixion of the only person who has ever lived a perfect life. Jesus Christ, God in the flesh, who was sent to earth for just one purpose: to die so that we could live. Even though it's obvious, this isn't a trite and trivial answer. This is the answer that changed the world from a place where evil wins to a place where evil is defeated. When God says, "The righteous shall live by his faith," he means that the way to get right with God is to put our faith in his Son and what he accomplished on the cross.

This is not the kind of solution to the problem of suffering and evil that we might expect. It certainly is not the answer offered by other religions and belief systems. Buddhism says that "detachment is the key to happiness."[8] Suffering and evil are eliminated when you get to a point when you no longer desire anything. Islam teaches that "suffering is atonement for one's wrongdoing."[9] The way to conquer pain is through martyrdom. Atheism is forced to explain why evil exists in the first place. If there is no God, there is no measure for good. If man is the measure, who's the judge of right and wrong if there's disagreement?

The honest truth is that people do have moral feelings, even moral *obligations*. "If there is no God, where do such strong moral instincts and feelings come from?" asks Keller.[10] When a skeptic or unbeliever declares something is evil, they are in fact confirming God's existence. For if God doesn't exist, then our certainty about good and evil ceases to exist as well. One opinion is as valid as the other. Of course, in order to maintain some semblance of order, someone or something with authority has to step into the godless vacuum and set its own standard of right and wrong. Usually that "something" is the state, and history is riddled with states that take the place of God with disastrous and, may we say, evil results.

The very fact that people are highly concerned about suffering and evil points to a God who has created a moral sense of right and wrong in all humanity. "The problem of senseless suffering does not go away if you abandon belief in God," writes Keller. "If there is no God, why have a sense of outrage and horror when unjust suffering occurs to any group of people?"[11]

QUESTIONS FOR REFLECTION AND DISCUSSION

- What is the most tragic thing that's ever happened in our world? What good came out of it?

- How do our moral obligations point to God's existence rather than deny it?
- Have you noticed an increase in moral outrage in our culture, even as belief in God has decreased? Can you explain why this is the case?

Our God Has Wounds

If we are outraged and horrified by suffering and evil, we can only imagine how God feels. In fact, we don't have to imagine. We can *know*. Christianity is not silent about the reality and nature of evil because God has spoken about it. When God told Habakkuk, "The righteous shall live by his faith," it wasn't a nice platitude. It was a statement of intent made by a God who would soon be sending his Son to earth for one purpose and one purpose only—to suffer and die so that we could live.

"The evil in human hearts nailed Christ to that cross," write McDowell and Morrow. "But God took our evil and redeemed it for good, the salvation of all who would trust him."[12]

Of all the world's belief systems, only Christianity tells the story of a God who has wounds.

We may wonder where God is when a great evil occurs somewhere in the world. We may question his goodness when a loved one is wracked with cancer or when we are going through a painful time in our life. Yes, God does care, and he demonstrated just how much when he sent Jesus to die for us (see Romans 5:8).

Why Does God Allow Suffering and Evil?

Earlier in this chapter, we talked about "approaches" rather than answers. We want to continue in that spirit as we consider possible reasons why God allows us to experience evil and to suffer rather than stop it. Here are two Bible verses and a quote from (who else) C. S. Lewis. After each verse and quote, indicate how you would approach the question, either verbally (if you're in a group) or by writing down your response.

> "You intended to harm me, but God intended it for good to accomplish what is now being done, the saving of many lives."
>
> Genesis 50:20

> That is why, for Christ's sake, I delight in weaknesses, in insults, in hardships, in persecutions, in difficulties. For when I am weak, then I am strong.
>
> 2 Corinthians 12:10

> God speaks to us in our pleasures, speaks in our conscience, but shouts in our pain: it is His megaphone to rouse a deaf world.
>
> C. S. Lewis[13]

God Is Being Patient

We'd like to offer one additional approach to the question of why God doesn't eliminate suffering and evil, one that comes from Joni Eareckson Tada. You may have heard of Joni. She's been a quadriplegic since she was paralyzed by a diving accident when she was seventeen years old. She's been confined to a wheelchair for more than half a century. As if her suffering wasn't enough, a few years ago Joni fought a battle with breast cancer.

Joni has suffered terribly in life, yet she has done some incredible things to help alleviate the suffering of others. In an interview with *Christianity Today* shortly after her ordeal with cancer, Joni answered the very same question we are asking in this chapter. Here's what she said:

> When people ask that question—even I struggle with that question—we aren't accepting the fact that this earth is wired to be difficult. The rule of thumb is that we experience much suffering because we live in a fallen world, and it is groaning under the weight

55

of a heavy curse. If God being good means that he has to get rid of sin, it means he would have to get rid of sinners. God is a God of great generosity and mercy, so he is keeping the execution of suffering. He's not closing the curtain on suffering until there is more time to gather more people into the fold of Christ's fellowship.[14]

Joni is echoing what Peter wrote to the first-century Christians, who were suffering badly under the oppressive treatment and persecution of the Romans. They were expecting Christ to return at any time and were getting frustrated that he wasn't rescuing them from the evil surrounding them. In a letter to the persecuted church, Peter gave them this reassurance:

The Lord is not slow in keeping his promise, as some understand slowness. Instead he is patient with you, not wanting anyone to perish, but everyone to come to repentance.

2 Peter 3:9

QUESTIONS FOR REFLECTION AND DISCUSSION

- What were your responses to the two verses (Genesis 50:20; 2 Corinthians 12:10) and the quote from Lewis?
- Explain what Joni Eareckson Tada means when she says, "God is a God of great generosity and mercy, so he is keeping the execution of suffering."

4

Why Is the Bible So Full of Violence?

Introduction

At the lunch break during a trial, two lawyers walked into a bar. (This is not the setup for a joke. It really happened. I [Bruce] was one of those lawyers.) No alcohol was consumed; we just required faster food service than was available in the restaurant. We promised each other that we wouldn't talk about the trial because we needed a momentary brain flush from the intense details of the case. The television on the wall displayed the top news story of the day, so that triggered a discussion about ISIS, which evolved into a more focused conversation about violent religious extremism. We both agreed it was a very bad thing. (See, sometimes lawyers can agree with each other.) But the compatibility of our viewpoints quickly dissipated (which probably confirms what you were thinking about lawyers in the first place).

My co-counsel knew that I was a Christian, and I now suspect that he lured me into the admission that "violent religious extremism is a very bad thing" with the premeditated purpose of beginning a cross-examination of my religious beliefs.

"If, as you say, horrific acts of brutality and bloodshed committed under the banner of religion are deplorable, then how can you claim allegiance to a God who condoned and commissioned such acts?" I wasn't afraid to engage in this sudden adversarial turn in the lunchtime conversation, but we were due back in court in eighteen minutes, so I told him to shut up and finish his chicken quesadilla.

The personality traits of my friend that make him a good litigator also, unfortunately, make him a difficult lunchtime companion. He was like a dog with a bone in its mouth; he wouldn't let go. So our oppositional banter continued for the next eighteen minutes. Later, during the remainder of the trial, he would pass to me notes on which he had scribbled attacks on . . .

- my powers of reasoning and logic: *Hey, Bruce, Exodus 20 says, "Thou shalt not kill." But 1 Samuel 15 says, "The Lord Almighty says . . . attack the Amalekites. . . . Do not spare them; put to death men and women, children and infants." How can you trust a God who is schizophrenic?*;
- my personal philosophies and worldview: *You say, "No God = No Peace"; I say, "Know God = Know Violence"*; and
- my anatomy: *How can you manage to walk around with your head up your butt?*

This chapter is dedicated to my fellow lawyer (whose identity will not be revealed because I'm sure he billed his client for the time he took to do some Bible research on his iPad and to scribble those notes during the trial).

The Bible Is Full of Violence. Can We Make Sense of It?

Violence seems to be integrally entwined with religion. This is true of most of the world's religions. There is savagery and brutality in the backstories even of those religions that have reputations for being tranquil and serene, like Buddhism[1] and Hinduism.[2] But the Bible, the sacred text of Christianity, seems to be the principal target of attacks and challenges in any discussion of violence in religion. Maybe deservedly so. After all, to a casual observer the Bible appears to be internally inconsistent and contradictory on this subject. The Bible's New Testament is jam-packed with "love your neighbor" stuff that sharply contrasts with the divinely commanded killing going on the Old Testament. In the best light, that is an apparent inconsistency. Under a more critical examination, it is hypocritical. Either way, it deserves an explanation, because this dichotomy puts in question the credibility of the Bible.

To those who are antagonistic opponents of Christianity, such as Richard Dawkins, no explanation could ever be acceptable or convincing. In his book *The God Delusion*, Dawkins states his position: "The ethnic cleansing begun in the time of Moses is brought to bloody fruition in the book of Joshua, a text remarkable for the bloodthirsty massacres it records and the xenophobic relish with which it does so."[3] That preconceived bias leads Dawkins to conclude that "the God of the Old Testament has got to be the most unpleasant character in all fiction."[4]

This chapter isn't addressed to Richard Dawkins. He would consider any explanation offered on the Christian perspective of the Bible to be illusory and fallacious because there would be disagreement about the *premise* of the explanation: Dawkins believes God is a fictional character; Christians believe that God is a real, living supreme being who has spoken through the Bible, which is entirely trustworthy. It is from that Christian premise that this chapter is written and offered to anyone who is making a genuine inquiry into the Christian faith. Your questions may not be satisfactorily answered, but hopefully we will come up with a basis to explain why Christians can read the violent descriptions in the Bible yet find God to be loving, just, and gracious.

QUESTIONS FOR REFLECTION AND DISCUSSION

- Do you have a preconceived bias (either for or against) about God?
- Do you have a bias about the subject of violence in the Bible?
- Can you accept the premise that God is real and that the Bible is true? If not, can you at least understand how Christians could subscribe to that premise?

Violence: Just Because It's in the Bible Doesn't Mean God Condones It

The Bible is unlike any other book. In fact, it is more like a compendium of sixty-six books, written over 1,600 years by forty authors, each of whom was divinely inspired by God as to what was written. Despite this collaborative effort that spanned centuries, there is a clearly conveyed overarching theme of the holy God's relentless pursuit to establish an intimate relationship with a sinful humanity. According to traditional groupings of the sixty-six books by category and style, there are . . .

- five books dealing with God's laws to the Hebrews;
- twelve books of Israel's early history;
- five books of poetry and wisdom;
- seventeen books containing the writings of the Old Testament prophets;
- four biographies of Jesus Christ;
- one book of history of the early Christian church;
- twenty-one letters (epistles) written to first-century Christians about doctrinal matters; and
- one book about prophecies of the end times.

When reading the Bible, we must respect these literary forms and context of the passage being read. For example:

- In his sermons, Jesus often emphasized points with the use of *parables* (allegories and fictional stories used by Jesus to illustrate a spiritual principle or lesson). The fact that the Bible contains some fictional stories in these parables does not invalidate the accuracy of the reported accounts presented in the Bible as historical fact. Many passages are accurate history. A few are hypothetical stories to illustrate a point. Some are descriptions of future events yet to happen at the time of writing. Others are personal letters containing encouragement; lessons about life, godliness, and doctrine; and admonishment. And some are poetry. You have to know which you are reading to properly understand the passage.

- Just because something is mentioned in the Bible doesn't make it holy. The Bible is not a giant how-to manual. Please don't think God wants you to emulate everything that is mentioned in the Bible. (Samson slew a thousand Philistines with the jawbone of a donkey; the prophet Ezekiel lay on his side for 390 days with a daily diet of dung sandwiches. We don't recommend that you engage in either of those activities; neither does the Bible.) Many of the biblical references are to behavior that should be *avoided* because such actions are offensive to God. A common biblical theme is God's grace and forgiveness to those who have sinned, as we see when some of the heroes of the Bible screwed up (like when Abraham lied about his marriage and allowed his wife to join Pharaoh's harem). The Bible's report of their sin shouldn't be viewed as God's permission for us to replicate their conduct.

We need to use these same principles of contextual reading as we examine the issue of violence in the Bible. There is a lot of wickedness described, and most of it should be directly attributed to the sinfulness of humanity, not to the desires or commands of God.

Understanding God: The Mandate of Holiness, Justice, and Righteousness

Humans have character traits. So does God, except that the theologians refer to them as God's *attributes*. These are the eternal, ever-present aspects of God's nature. The most famous one is *love*, as in "God is love" (1 John 4:8). Other attributes relevant to this discussion reveal that

- God is holy (see 1 Peter 1:15),
- God is just (see 2 Thessalonians 1:6), and
- God is righteous (see Psalm 145:17).

It is difficult to distinguish between God's holiness and his righteousness, and references to God's justice and his righteousness are often used synonymously. There is overlap and interplay among them:

> God's righteousness (or justice) is a natural expression of His holiness. If He is infinitely pure, then He must be opposed to all sin, and that opposition to sin must be demonstrated in His treatment of His creatures. When we read that God is righteous or just, we are being assured that His actions toward us are in perfect agreement with His holy nature.[5]

An accurate assessment of the violent acts by God hurled down upon humanity as reported in the Old Testament requires a contextual understanding of God's attributes (especially his holiness, justice, and righteousness). In the process of such a consideration, what might seem like an ill-tempered, random act of violence may be better understood as a patient, appropriate exercise of God's righteous response to wickedness. Our poor analogy: assuming child abuse when you see a parent yank a toddler by the arm, only to learn later that the stern treatment saved the child from stepping off the curb and being hit by an approaching car. A better real-life illustration: the destruction of Sodom and Gomorrah. Read the entire story in Genesis 18:1–19:29; here's our abridged bullet-point summary:

- The depravity and debauchery in the neighboring cities of Sodom and Gomorrah is rampant and unabated. The "outcry against Sodom and Gomorrah is so great and their sin so grievous" that God decides to make a personal inspection visit. (God is omniscient—he knows everything—so he doesn't need to make the interstellar trip. But doing so demonstrates to Abraham, and to us, that God doesn't act rashly; his decisions are based on his personal knowledge and applied in a just manner.)
- God appears in physical form (with two angels) at the encampment of Abraham, who mistakes the trio for travelers. Abraham invites them to stay for a chat, during which time God gives a clue about his divinity by prophesying that ninety-year-old Sarah will get pregnant.
- Abraham is told that God intends to visit Sodom (where Abraham's nephew, Lot, and his family live) to assess the situation there. God doesn't need to disclose these details to Abraham, but God wants to use this occasion for teaching Abraham, and us, about "doing righteousness and justice" (ESV).
- When Abraham hears God's plan, he is afraid God will obliterate both cities. He begins to intercede on behalf of the residents (which include his kinfolk). He argues that a just

God couldn't destroy the cities if virtuous people were living there among the wicked. He negotiates with God to spare the cities if fifty righteous people can be found in Sodom's population.

- Sensing God's willingness, Abraham keeps squeezing God to lower the threshold (from fifty to forty-five, to forty, to thirty, then to twenty). He gets God down to as few as ten: If ten righteous people can be found in Sodom, the cities are spared. It's a deal.

- But Abraham has vastly overestimated the moral segment of the population (apparently incorrectly assuming that his nephew would have had at least a modest positive influence). Only four people who meet the qualification (Lot, his wife, and their two daughters) are found in Sodom.

- God, as a matter of righteousness, could annihilate everyone because ten are not found. But in his sense of justice God allows Lot and his family to escape to a nearby town, after which God rains down burning sulfur on Sodom and Gomorrah. The next morning, Abraham looks out in the distance where Sodom and Gomorrah used to be; all he can see is "dense smoke rising from the land, like smoke from a furnace."

This is one of many instances in the book of Genesis where God revealed his righteousness and justice specifically for Abraham and his descendants. God wanted to make his character known, and he wanted those traits to be reproduced in the lives of Abraham and his lineal descendants (who, in future years, became the Israelites, God's chosen people).

The more we understand about God's holiness, the more we may realize why he finds sin so deplorable. The more we know about God's righteousness, the more we may realize why he finds sin so intolerable. And the more we comprehend what it means for God to be just, then the more we may consider his judgments to be appropriate. We can't understand the *why* of God's judgments until we absorb the *what* of God's nature. A. W. Tozer stated that our criticism of God's judgments are the result of "several deep-lying misconceptions":

> These have to do with the holiness of God, the nature of man, the gravity of sin, and the awesome wonder of the love of God as expressed in redemption. Whoever understands these even imperfectly will take God's side forever, and whatever He may do they will cry with the voice out of the altar, "Yes, Lord God Almighty, true and just are your judgments" (Revelation 16:7).[6]

QUESTIONS FOR REFLECTION AND DISCUSSION

- Describe some aspect of God's character as you understand it.
- Is there some feature of God's personality that you are unsure about?
- Do you agree that there is a causal connection between God's attributes and his actions that should be considered when evaluating God's violent acts as reported in the Bible? Explain your answer.

God's Wrath: Does God Go Wild, or Is He Always in Control?

Even if we understand the rules of literary and contextual application, and even if we attempt to comprehend the enormity of God's holiness, the graphic description of God's judgment poured out on hapless (but evil) humans points to what sometimes seems like an overreaction on God's part. After all, isn't he a "God of second chances"? (Isn't there a verse about that? Or maybe we are just thinking of a country-western song lyric.) Your bottom-line question might be "Couldn't God have been a little more humane in the dispensation of his judgment?" Put more succinctly, "What's the deal with all the wrath?" Here's a quick answer: God is a lot of things, but he is not politically correct.

God's wrath is at the heart of people's objection to the display of God's judgment in the Old Testament. There is no denying it. It pops off the pages. Christians in the twenty-first century are often uncomfortable with this. From their contemporary societal perspective, *wrath* seems a bit uncouth; it's passé; we've evolved beyond such primitive emotions. In a culture that worships *tolerance*, wrath is out of place.

But God's capacity for wrath is in his nature. And it is going to stay there. God is immutable; he is the same yesterday, today, and tomorrow; he does not change. And that is a good thing for us, because we don't need to worry about him making arbitrary rule changes with respect to our salvation.

A. W. Pink was a famous Bible teacher who lived from 1886 to 1952. Even during that time, Christians were getting squeamish with the subject of God's wrath:

> It is sad to find so many professing Christians who appear to regard the wrath of God as something for which they need to make an apology, or at least they wish there were no such thing. While some would not go so far as to openly admit that they consider it a blemish on the Divine character, yet they are far from regarding it with delight; they like not to think about it, and they rarely hear it mentioned without a secret resentment rising up in their hearts against it. . . . [Yet] many there are who turn away from a vision of God's wrath as though they were called to look upon some blotch in the Divine character, or some blot upon the Divine government. But what saith the Scriptures? As we turn to them we find that God has made no attempt to conceal the fact of His wrath. He is not ashamed to make it known that vengeance and fury belong unto Him.[7]

A definition will be helpful at this point. God's wrath is never hot-tempered, retaliatory, or out-of-control anger. Quite the contrary. Whenever God unleashes his wrath, it is controlled, deliberate, proportional, and justified. A. W. Pink defines it in this way:

The wrath of God is His eternal detestation of all unrighteousness. It is the displeasure and indignation of Divine equity against evil. It is the holiness of God stirred into activity against sin. It is the moving cause of that just sentence which He passes upon evil-doers. God is angry against sin because it is a rebelling against His authority, a wrong done to His inviolable sovereignty. Insurrectionists against God's government shall be made to know that God is the Lord. They shall be made to feel how great that Majesty is which they despise, and how dreadful is that threatened wrath which they so little regarded. Not that God's anger is a malignant and malicious retaliation, inflicting injury for the sake of it, or in return for injury received. No; while God will vindicate His dominion as Governor of the universe, He will not be vindictive.[8]

Because God's wrath is a divine response arising from his holiness and sense of justice, the Bible doesn't downplay the acts of God's wrath; it highlights them. Readers of the Old Testament are captivated (and/or repulsed) by the brutality, so much so that they often miss the narrative that explains the impetus that triggered God's righteous indignation. So you will read that God's wrath was meted out upon a person or group, but there is always an accompanying explanation of the underlying cause. For example, look at some instances of when God's wrath befell these people:

The inhabitants of the world: As reported in Genesis 7, the great flood covered the earth and killed all but eight of its inhabitants (the survivors being Noah and his family). But previously, in Genesis 6, God saw "how great the wickedness of the human race had become on the earth, and that every inclination of the thoughts of the human heart was only evil all the time" (verse 5). God waited patiently during the nearly one hundred years it took Noah to build the ark (see 1 Peter 3:20), but no one heeded the warnings given to Noah (see Hebrews 11:7).

Some of his own chosen people: Moses was in charge of the children of Israel during the forty years they wandered in the wilderness. Four malcontents gathered a group of 250 who challenged Moses' leadership and the delegation of responsibilities.

There was a nonviolent confrontation, but the next day the ground under the four men "split apart and the earth opened its mouth and swallowed them and their households. . . . They went down alive into the realm of the dead, with everything they owned; the earth closed over them, and they perished and were gone from the community" (Numbers 16:31–33). And as for the 250 followers, "fire came out from the Lord and consumed the 250 men." Yes, it sounds harsh, but these men challenged the God-ordained authority of Moses; worse than that, they had gathered "against the Lord" as they plotted their mutiny. It was a rebellion against the Lord and a blatant refusal of submission. God gave them a chance to recant when Moses warned that "it is against the Lord that you and all your followers have banded together" (verse 11), but they remained defiant . . . all the way to the center of the earth.

The Canaanite city of Jericho: When the children of Israel entered the Promised Land, God commanded them to conquer all of the nation groups within the region. Except for the Canaanities, the Israelites were to approach each city with an offer of peace before engaging. This is in addition to the time that God had given for these nations to repent. With respect to the Canaanite city-states, God specifically ordered that all of the cities and residents be destroyed. They had long engaged in such vile religious rituals as temple prostitution and child sacrifices. God realized that the Canaanites, as a whole, were a threat to the survival of the Israelites. The first Canaanite city the Israelites approached was Jericho—with its fortified walls that were virtually impenetrable. God's battle plan was too simplistic to be threatening, but it was entirely effective: March around the city, blow your trumpets, and the walls will fall down. And that's exactly what happened. But some people, like Richard Dawkins, read the following passage from Joshua and immediately see a type of ethnic cleansing in what happened after the collapse of the walls:

> [The Israelites] charged straight in, and they took the city. They
> devoted the city to the Lord and destroyed with the sword every

living thing in it—men and women, young and old, cattle, sheep and donkeys.

Joshua 6:20–22

Admittedly, the killing at Jericho reminds us of acts of twenty-first century militant religious terrorists. But a closer reading of the Jericho story shows that God was making efforts to save those in the city who were God-fearing. Four chapters earlier in the story, the Israelite spies who did reconnaissance inside the city walls were almost captured. They were protected by a heroic woman, Rahab, who was a prostitute in Jericho. She hid the spies, at great risk to the safety of herself and her family, and helped them escape. She explained her motivation to the spies by saying, "The Lord your God is God in heaven above and on the earth below" (Joshua 4:11). Consequently, this battle had nothing to do with ethnic cleansing; it had everything to do with allegiance to or defiance of the one true God.

As these stories reveal, wherever the Bible reports God's wrath, it always explains the righteous context that necessitated it.

QUESTIONS FOR REFLECTION AND DISCUSSION

- Does the backstory in the three biblical accounts change your opinion of whether God's wrath was righteous or irrational?
- Are there other biblical events that are troubling to your sensitivity of justice? Have you examined those passages to see if there is an explanation that reveals God's righteousness?

The Old Testament: Explained and Amplified by the New Testament

A cursory reading of the Bible might have you asking, "How come God goes hog wild with wrath in the Old Testament, but then turns loving and caring in the New Testament?" That's the common understanding of Scripture, but we respectfully submit that

69

the weight of evidence for God's wrath resides in the New Testament. Theologian D. A. Carson makes the observation that the Old Testament foreshadows the nature of both God's love and God's wrath, but the magnitude of both his love and wrath are more clearly presented in the New Testament:

> The reality is that the Old Testament displays *the grace and love of God* in experience and types, and these realities become all the clearer in the New Testament. Similarly, the Old Testament displays *the righteous wrath of God* in experience and types, and these realities become all the clearer in the New Testament. In other words both God's love and God's wrath are ratcheted up in the move from the Old Testament to the New. These themes barrel along through redemptive history, unresolved, until they come to a resounding climax in the Cross.[9]

God's righteousness is not a lame excuse that is used to rationalize his use of violence. His righteousness is so sincere, so intense, and so implacable that God's wrath, in full measure, was directed at his Son on the cross. There is no greater violence found in the pages of the Bible than the brutality suffered by Christ on the cross. Not only did he suffer physical pain, torture and death, but he also endured spiritual destruction and death, separating him from the love of his Father.

And, in the midst of the horror of the cross, we also see the greatest act of love ever displayed as the perfect, sinless Christ endured the atrocities of the cross in self-sacrifice for a rebellious, ungrateful, immoral human race.

Carson condenses this paradoxical confluence of wrath and love into two sentences:

> Do you wish to see God's love? Look at the Cross.
> Do you wish to see God's wrath? Look at the Cross.[10]

The Bible is replete with evidence of violence emanating from God's righteous wrath. What you'll find of it in the Old Testament is explained by what you'll read of it in the New Testament.

QUESTIONS FOR REFLECTION AND DISCUSSION

- How does a single event—the crucifixion of Christ—reveal both the wrath of God and the love of God?
- How does God's holiness play into the scene?
- Why is humanity's sinfulness relevant?
- Recall the opinions you had about Old Testament violence before you read this chapter. Do your thoughts about the crucifixion of Christ change those previously held opinions?

5

Does God Care That the World Is Falling Apart?

Introduction

Blogger Amy Hall once described an interaction she had with another woman via Twitter. The woman railed against Amy's belief in God, stating, "You clearly have never had a time when you were hurt. I don't mean sick. I don't mean heart broken. I mean literally a near-death experience or rape or abusive relationship. . . . You can keep floating on a [expletive] cloud thinking Jesus will do everything for you but it's a lie."[1]

A terrible and painful experience fueled this woman's anger. As they interacted through the Twitterverse, Amy learned the woman had been raped, and that "her trauma had played a central role in her becoming an outspoken, obviously angry 'antitheist.'"[2]

As authors, we won't pretend to fully understand the pain caused by this tragic, harmful, and unjust crime. But she seems convinced that Christianity teaches that "Jesus will do everything for you." She has gleaned from one source or another an inaccurate portrayal of Christianity, and the results are wrong answers to important questions amid her very terrible trials. In her response to Amy's tweet, you can almost hear her pleading with God, asking him if he cares. *God, she might be wondering, do you even care about all the pain, heartbreak, terror, and abuse I have suffered?*

She's not alone. Many people ask if God cares. Personal experiences and the barrage of bad news splashed across our TVs and smartphone screens have us convinced the world is falling apart. And with the exception of the most jaded and self-absorbed, we care. We care deeply. The question many have is "Does *God* care?"

Not the First

Have you ever become so familiar with a story that it doesn't seem real anymore? This can happen with the Bible and the events it records. If we're not careful, we can forget that it's fact, not fiction. The folks who followed Moses, listened to the prophets, were healed by Jesus, or were taught by Paul were real people. They lived at a real time in real places. They had birthdays and anniversaries, families and friends, hopes and fears, likes and dislikes. They were people, just like us.

They, too, must have wrestled with questions about suffering and evil, right? There were no paperback books like this one, but we can rest assured they sought out opportunities to question, talk to, and argue with God and others about these very same issues. And thankfully, the Bible never sugarcoats it. The authors of Scripture simply recorded it. In the Bible's pages we see real people just like us asking real questions just like us.

Lamentations is an entire book of the Bible devoted to the expression of sorrow. The psalmists were never afraid of calling out to God. In Psalm 61:1–2, King David wrote, "Hear my cry, O God; listen to my prayer. From the ends of the earth I call to you, I call as my heart grows faint." But they did more than just cry out when the world was not right. The psalmists wondered, just like we do, if God really cares. And they were bold enough to say so! Here's one example of a psalmist's unfiltered words:

> "O God my rock," I cry, "Why have you forgotten me? Why must I wander around in grief, oppressed by my enemies?" Their taunts break my bones. They scoff, "Where is this God of yours?"
>
> Psalm 42:9–10 NLT

Elijah, a prophet of God, was sent by God to the city of Zarephath, where he stayed with a widow and her son. While in their care, the boy grew ill and died. What did Elijah do and say?

> "Give me your son," Elijah replied. He took him from her arms, carried him to the upper room where he was staying, and laid him on his bed. Then he cried out to the Lord, "Lord my God, have you brought tragedy even on this widow I am staying with, by causing her son to die?"
>
> 1 Kings 17:19–20

Here's one more example from the Old Testament. It's another prophet's prayer in a time of great need and trouble.

> How long, Lord, must I call for help, but you do not listen? Or cry out to you, "Violence!" but you do not save? Why do you make me look at injustice? Why do you tolerate wrongdoing? Destruction and violence are before me; there is strife, and conflict abounds.
>
> Habakkuk 1:2–3

Passionate inquiry about God's love and care amid suffering and evil is not only an Old Testament phenomenon. The great missionary and evangelist Paul described his persistent ailment as "a thorn in [his] flesh, a messenger of Satan." Then he wrote, "Three times I pleaded with the Lord to take it away from me" (2 Corinthians 12:7–8). He also must have wondered if God cared about his pain.

Last but certainly not least, Jesus himself cried out to God in his suffering. Jesus was brutally tortured. His enemies drove nails through his flesh to hang him for death on two planks of wood.

Understandably, Jesus cried out to God. In a moment when original words and thoughts were impossible to muster, Jesus recited David's pained questions from Psalm 22. The Bible says, "About three in the afternoon Jesus cried out in a loud voice, . . . 'My God, my God, why have you forsaken me?'" (Matthew 27:46). These words—this question for God—were Jesus' dying breath.

These examples from God's very Word show that we are not alone. In fact, we're in very good company! Everyone wonders about God's love for us when we are in such deep strife and pain. There must be a better way, we think. Surely God is paying attention, we hope. We wonder, *Does God care about me and this world? If God is real, why does he seem so distant?*

QUESTIONS FOR REFLECTION AND DISCUSSION

- Have you ever asked these questions before? What circumstances led to them?
- What do you think and feel when you discover that real people throughout the Bible wrestled with God over these same issues?
- Do you relate to them? Do you relate to Amy Hall's reader from the introduction? If so, how?

A Distant God

There's a name for the belief in a distant God. It's called deism. Here are two definitions for those not yet familiar with the term:

> Belief in the existence of a supreme being, specifically of a creator who does not intervene in the universe. The term is used chiefly of an intellectual movement of the 17th and 18th centuries that accepted the existence of a creator on the basis of reason but rejected belief in a supernatural deity who interacts with humankind.[3]

> Belief in a God who created the world but has since remained indifferent to it.[4]

In other words, deism posits that God is an inventor, but not the mechanic. The implications of this are fairly easy to apprehend. A distant God does not care about the actions of people. This God is incapable of, or uninterested in, personal dealings with the humans his invention spawned. The distant God of deism is unknowable and neither listens to nor speaks to his creation.

This kind of God is very powerful, but he isn't particularly present. This God is creative, but not compassionate. He/she/it is a grand initiator but has no follow-through.

This poses a question for those interested in Christianity. Is the deity of deism the same as the God of Christianity? In what kind of God, exactly, do Christians believe and give their lives?

A Close God (in Scripture)

The comparison between deism (or any belief system) and Christianity is an important one. The truth is that Christianity claims something much, much different from what deism claims. The one and only belief they share is that God is responsible for the beginning of everything. Outside of that, the differences are stark.

The writers of the Bible clearly communicate that God is no disengaged deity. He is a God of close encounters. Here are some key Bible verses that help us understand why Christians believe God is not far away:

- *Genesis tells us God physically walked with his new creation.* "When the cool evening breezes were blowing, the man and his wife heard the Lord God walking about in the garden" (Genesis 3:8 NLT).

- *God met personally with Moses, his appointed leader of Israel.* "Inside the Tent of Meeting, the Lord would speak to Moses face to face, as one speaks to a friend" (Exodus 33:11 NLT).

- *King David wrote about the closeness of God in one of his most famous psalms.* "Even though I walk through the darkest valley, I will fear no evil, for you are with me" (Psalm 23:4).

- *The incarnation—God in human form—is by definition a close encounter with God.* "The virgin will conceive and give birth to a son, and they will call him Immanuel (which means 'God with us')" (Matthew 1:23).

- *Jesus promises to be remarkably close to all who seek and trust him.* "Remain in me, and I will remain in you" (John 15:4 NLT).

- *Even after Jesus' ascension (see Acts 1), he is present with us in the Holy Spirit.* "Don't you know that you yourselves are God's temple and that God's Spirit dwells in your midst?" (1 Corinthians 3:16).

Have you ever met someone famous? Our friend Kim is a huge fan of a particular professional football team. Her close friend is related to one of the well-known and talented members of the team. One night Kim's friend surprised her by bringing this football star and Super Bowl champion to her house for dinner! Kim was beside herself. One of her favorite players from her favorite team was at her dinner table. She struggled to believe it was actually happening.

That's just a football player. A human being. Imagine if God stopped by for dinner!

The very idea of God being present with us (with us!) is mind-blowing. God is infinitely more important, more powerful, more talented, and much more famous than any one person. He's God. And the Bible makes it clear that he is close and that we can experience him in deeply personal ways.

The clearest example is Jesus, God's own Son, who walked the earth as a man. The Gospel of John states it like this: "In the beginning was the Word, and the Word was with God, and the Word was God" (John 1:1). The "Word" in this instance is referring to

Jesus. John then says, "The Word [Jesus] became flesh and made his dwelling among us. We have seen his glory, the glory of the one and only Son, who came from the Father, full of grace and truth" (John 1:14).

God's closeness in Jesus was physical like never before. But he also closed the emotional gap between us and God. Jesus experienced human reality firsthand. He knows personally the intricacies of our difficulties and trials.

The Bible says Jesus wept (see John 11:35); Jesus was hungry (see Mark 11:12) and thirsty (see John 19:28); Jesus was tempted (see Matthew 4:1–11); Jesus was insulted (see Luke 22:63–65); Jesus was tortured, hated, and cruelly murdered (see the last third of each Gospel).

The author of Hebrews referred to Jesus when he wrote this: "For we do not have a high priest [Jesus] who is unable to empathize with our weaknesses, but we have one who has been tempted in every way, just as we are—yet he did not sin" (Hebrews 4:15). The apostle Paul wrote about Jesus' humanness in poignant terms.

> In your relationships with one another, have the same mindset as Christ Jesus: Who, being in very nature God, did not consider equality with God something to be used to his own advantage; rather, he made himself nothing by taking the very nature of a servant, being made in human likeness. And being found in appearance as a man, he humbled himself by becoming obedient to death—even death on a cross!
>
> Philippians 2:5–8

The God of Christianity does not stay far away. Quite the opposite. Jesus—God in the flesh—shows that the Christian faith is far from deism. God is not content to set the world spinning, and then go and find another hobby. He loves his creation. All of it. He loves you. All of you. And he wants to be intimately connected through a real, meaningful, and thriving relationship that brings greater joy than you've ever imagined. He also longs to reveal himself, not just through Jesus, but through the Holy Spirit's presence and work in your life this very day.

A Close God (in Modern Day)

I (Chris) am an assistant pastor and lead a few different ministries. I work diligently (with God's help, thankfully) to identify leaders who are called by God to lead each ministry. Those leaders come from a random smattering of backgrounds, ages, life circumstances, and faith experiences.

Recently I sat with a new set of leaders. We explored our faith stories by sharing what life was like before following Jesus, how we became a Christian, and what life is like as a follower of Jesus today. Though unique and varied, each story had one thing in common: God supernaturally revealed himself to every single person. He met us all, exactly where we were, at some point in our journey. For these faithful followers of Jesus, God is not some cherished idea, deferred hope, or unrealized wish. He is someone they know. God had come close to them. He was—and still is—close to them.

We've experienced the same in the Alpha course, a ten-week experience designed for the unchurched in which a small group of people gather to share a meal, hear a talk about one aspect of life and the Christian faith, and then discuss it openly and honestly. It's a refreshing and impacting way to engage the gospel with our unbelieving friends and community in an open, welcoming, nonjudgmental setting—kind of like these books of ours.

In week two of the Alpha experience, the topic is "Who is Jesus?" In the explanation of who Jesus is, the video presentation describes how there are a couple billion Christians from every country, every ethnicity, every economic, social, and intellectual background in the world. The presenters then point out that the world's Christians "all speak of this encounter with the risen Jesus Christ."[5]

Christians who live out their faith through prayer, worship of God, learning the Bible, and living life with a believing community consistently talk about the supernatural presence, power, and peace of God in their lives. Somehow it is far more than just an intellectual apprehension of facts or a blindly held set of beliefs. They swear that God is with them—not far away—and their personal experience is tangible.

Does this seem like the kind of impact a distant deity would have? According to the Bible's description of God and people's firsthand experiences with him, the God who created the cosmos is the same God who walks with his people day in and day out.

When it comes to our suffering and pain, if God is as close as Christianity and Christians say that he is, is he more likely to be a God who cares, or a God who could not care less? Christianity teaches that he is a close-by God precisely because he cares a great deal.

QUESTIONS FOR REFLECTION AND DISCUSSION

- Is it better to have a God who is far off, or God who is close-by? What are the benefits of each? The downsides?
- What are your first thoughts when you hear someone tell of an experience with God?
- Have you encountered God's presence? When? Where? What was it like?
- If you haven't experienced God's presence, would you like to? Why or why not?

Then Why Doesn't He *Do* Something?

We once heard a story about a young aspiring police officer who was completing his final exams in the academy. The first few questions were relatively easy, but then he reached question number four:

> Imagine you are on patrol when a gas main under a nearby street explodes. As you run to the scene, you see an overturned van with a

man and woman inside. Both are injured and reek of alcohol. You recognize the woman as the wife of your commanding officer who happens to be traveling out of the country. A man on a motorcycle stops to offer help, but when he removes his helmet, you realize his identity: a man wanted for armed robbery. Suddenly another man runs out of a nearby house shouting that his wife is nine months pregnant and the explosion has sent her into labor. Another man is yelling for help after being blown by the explosion into an adjacent canal and cannot swim.

Describe in a few words the actions you would take.

As the story goes, the officer thought for a moment, and then wrote his short but telling answer: *I would take off my uniform and mingle with the crowd.*

Sometimes it feels as though God has taken off his "God uniform" and disappeared into the crowd in times of obvious and overwhelming need. If God truly is close-by, then we want—and expect—more of him. If he's God, then we expect him to rescue the couple from the burning van, tell the motorcyclist how to save the drowning man, then run into the house and deliver a perfectly healthy baby.

Honestly, many of us also expect God to remedy every emotional and social problem as well as the physical ones (and by "remedy" we often mean "forgive and forget"). We want God to keep the woman's secret from her husband, overlook their drinking and driving, and let the armed robber off the hook. After all, it's easier to believe these are desperate victims, not sinful people.

Our cry to God in the midst of so much tragedy and destruction, sin, and death is simple and loud. "Why don't you *do* something!?!?" If God is so close and if he cares so much, why doesn't he stop all the pain?

This is one of the most difficult questions all Christians face. As we have already noted, the existence of suffering and evil is the primary roadblock to faith for many people. In our minds a good God would grant constant comfort, safety, and health. A good God would halt the bad guys, enable the good guys, and fix all problems with the snap of his fingers.

Like you, we struggle with the same questions and desire. On a personal or relational level, we have faced cancer, financial loss, broken relationships, chronic pain, fear, doubt, uncertainty, loneliness, depression, and death. And that's just the three of us! We know that you—our readers—have endured a vast array of suffering and pain. Some of you are in the throes of it right now. And it is difficult to see a way out. You might wonder if God is close at all.

Because we've been there, we won't give flippant answers. Instead, in response to this question—"Why doesn't he do something?"—we offer a few other questions. This is a series of books about wrestling with the toughest questions, after all. And we've found that sometimes, new questions can help us wrestle with old questions better than a set of pat answers. Ironically, with more questions we often find fresh perspective and new strains of hope.

Is It Good That God Doesn't Eliminate Evil?

Much of the world's pain, injury, and sorrow results from humans acting against other humans. Is it possible that God will not prohibit sin on a personal scale because doing so would inhibit his love on a grand scale? (Refer back to chapter 1 for more on this question.) Is it possible that God cares so deeply for all of us that he refuses to violate anyone's freedom by making our harmful choices and actions impossible?

Are we doing our part to solve the problem?

Just as people are responsible for much of the world's pain, we are also responsible for its healing. God's design for a thriving world has always included people (us!). To what degree does God ask us to help solve the problem of suffering and evil? Do we ignore or delegate important, lifesaving work because we'd rather stay blissfully unaware of the world's pain? Because we don't want to leave our comfort zone? Because we're lazy? Are people suffering more than they should because we don't care for them like we should? And how much good are we missing out on because we don't let God use us to help?

Do we value what God values?

This question is difficult for our enlightened, Western, secularly influenced minds to truly grapple with. But it must be asked. Is it possible that our comfort, health, and pleasure are not God's highest values? Could the old cliché be true: No pain, no gain? Is it wrong for God to allow us pain if we become stronger, wiser, more compassionate, and less selfish, and experience greater joy because of it? Is it possible that God values something that is only attainable through suffering? And is it possible that we would be better off if we valued what he values?

Don't nonchalantly toss these questions out in a grief support group or to a feisty bunch of atheists. They won't likely win you any favor. But if we truly want to honestly engage with God—the good, loving, powerful, kind, and noble God who created this universe—we must wrestle with these kinds of questions. And we must do so with humility, remembering these words God spoke through his prophet Isaiah: "'For my thoughts are not your thoughts, neither are your ways my ways,' declares the Lord. 'As the heavens are higher than the earth, so are my ways higher than your ways and my thoughts than your thoughts'" (Isaiah 55:8–9).

We are limited in our ability to fully understand the mind of God. Therefore, we are limited in understanding all the ways in which his creation works. But these questions—even the ones we'd rather never know the answer to—can help us.

QUESTIONS FOR REFLECTION AND DISCUSSION

- Do you ever feel like God has abandoned his post?
- When have you asked God the question "Why don't you *do* something?" What happened?

> • How does our list of questions help or hurt your quest to discover if God cares about your (or the world's) suffering?

God Has Done Something

We might never fully know the mind of God, but we are very thankful we can know enough. And we are certain of this: God has definitively answered the question "Does God care that the world is falling apart?" We know that not every person will find God's answer satisfying. If everyone did, everyone would be a Christian! But God has answered. And that answer is the crux of Christianity.

So what is his answer to this vital question? Jesus.

Jesus' life, death, resurrection, ascension, and promised return are proof that God cares deeply about our crumbling world and the suffering we endure. Out of God's good grace, Jesus has given us what every sufferer needs.

Empathy

As we pointed out above, Jesus fully experienced real human life. His body was real. He was born, he grew, and he aged. He experienced all the good things in life: family, friendships, work, worship, food, drink, and celebrations. He was also intimately acquainted with the worst of life. He was abandoned, betrayed, abused physically and emotionally. He knew loneliness, hunger and thirst, ostracism, and ridicule. He even died. You name it, Jesus experienced it. Are you suffering? He's been there, and he's here now.

Presence

Sufferers also need companionship. Randy Alcorn, the author of *The Goodness of God*, wrote, "God doesn't just offer us advice, he offers us companionship. He doesn't promise we won't face hardship, but he does promise he'll walk with us through our

85

hardship."[6] God cares so much that he is here, now. If you are a Christian—if you have recognized God's love, confessed your sin, accepted God's forgiveness, and trusted your life to him—then by the power of the Holy Spirit God is with you and in you at this very moment. If you are not a Christian, God is still fully available to you. He's there, ready for you to acknowledge him and allow him to become even closer with you.

Emotional restoration

Because Jesus has made a way for us to know and experience God himself, we can be restored emotionally. Jesus gives—and shows us how to have—peace of mind and heart, even amid physical stress, discomfort, and pain.

Physical restoration

Jesus heals. He always has. The Gospels overflow with accounts of Jesus' supernatural restoration of the blind, lame, diseased, and possessed. Miraculously, those stories still abound as God continues to heal today. Not everyone is healed in this life. Death comes to everyone. But for those in Christ, death is simply a doorway to ultimate healing.

Spiritual restoration

In the end, a spiritual cure is more important than emotional or physical remedies. We most need to know that despite our sin, a restored relationship with God is possible. And that—more than anything else—is what Jesus accomplished.

God cares so deeply about his broken, dark, and dying world that he sent his own Son to fix it. Jesus said, "Greater love has no one than this: to lay down one's life for one's friends" (John 15:13). This is more than a quotable line. It's the life Jesus lived. The Son of God died a dreadful death and endured excruciating separation from God so we wouldn't have to. After living the perfect life we could never live, he died the death we deserve to die, and then walked out of the grave we could never escape on our own. And in so doing he initiated a world-renewing movement that we can participate in and enjoy. He made an emotionally, physically, and spiritually healed life possible. And it's all been done because he loves us.

So does God care that the world is falling apart? Yes. He cares very much. He gave his very life for it. Could he care any more?

QUESTIONS FOR REFLECTION AND DISCUSSION

- What do you think and feel about Jesus? Does he help answer the question "Does God care?" Why or why not?
- Is it helpful to know that God understands your pain?
- Have you ever felt restored by Jesus in any way, shape, or form? If not, would you like to?
- God loves you. He cares about your pain. Will you respond to his love? How?

6

Why Do the Innocent Suffer?

Introduction

We first met Makoto Fujimura in New York City. We were traveling the country doing research for a book, *Bruce & Stan Search for the Meaning of Life*. At the time Mako was a relatively unknown Japanese-American artist who was bringing new meaning and credibility to beautiful works of art being created by Christians in the nation's cultural capital. Mako was born in America but spent his formative years in Japan, where he studied at the University of the Arts in Tokyo. Today his images, which he paints using the ancient Japanese practice of *Nihonga*, are world renowned.

In the summer of 2000, we interviewed Mako in his studio in lower Manhattan, just blocks from the terrorist attacks that would take place a year later. Fifteen months after America's Ground Zero shocked the world, Mako stood atop Martyrs Hill in Nagasaki, a mile from Japan's own Ground Zero, where the atomic bomb was dropped in August 1945. There are twenty-six crosses on Martyrs Hill, memorializing something that took place in Nagasaki three and a half centuries before the atomic bomb.

In 1597, at the beginning of a period of persecution against Japanese Christians that was to last 250 years, twenty-six men and three children were marched 480 miles from Kyoto to the hill in Nagasaki to be crucified as a way of stopping the growth of Christianity in feudal Japan. Their ears and noses had been cut off so that they would be humiliated and taunted on the journey. When they arrived, bleeding and helpless, crosses were already lined up, ready for their crucifixions. The story has it that one of the children, an eleven-year-old boy, said, "Show me my cross." Another boy echoed, "Show me mine." Mako explains how he felt as he visited Martyrs Hill that day in 2002:

> I stood there, trying to imagine what they experienced, and for a moment their suffering seemed incalculable to me. Like the beaded stained-glass windows, droplets of melted church on the ashes of Ground Zero, these two small crosses point to the stoic surrender of the Japanese souls that is reflected in the deaths of the martyrs. I thought about the chaos and uncertainty of my own Ground Zero experience in New York City, but this, obviously, was the beginning of a great trauma that went beyond any of my own experiences.[1]

Incalculable Suffering

Even though they took place in another place and another time, stories like the one from Martyrs Hill elicit feelings of grief and sadness. We have not been to Japan's Ground Zero, but we have experienced two other sobering reminders of the evil in our world: the 9/11 Memorial and Museum in New York City, and the haunting Holocaust memorial in Jerusalem known as Yad Vashem. Both of these places are designed to tell the stories of human suffering that occurred as a result of horrific events—so that we don't forget what happened. We don't possess Makoto Fujimura's ability to express in words or in art the effect of these encounters on our senses, but we know how it feels to witness the ghastly experience of innocent lives taken by forces they never expected.

Mako's description of "incalculable suffering" seems right. We can't know, we can't measure, and we can't imagine what it's like to be treated like the men and children crucified for their beliefs on Martyrs Hill. It would be one thing if such unspeakable cruelties were a thing of the past, but we know that's not the way it is. Incalculable suffering is happening now, in our time, in our world. We can't imagine what it was like for those twenty-one Egyptian Coptic Christians who were lined up and beheaded because they refused to renounce their faith in Christ. We agonize when we hear about hundreds of schoolgirls kidnapped in Nigeria by terrorists who enslave them for months if not years.

By God's grace or sheer determination (or maybe a little of both), we seem better equipped to handle the suffering in our own lives, whether it happens to us personally or to a friend or family member. Because we're close to it, we have ways of dealing with the pain. We don't often feel helpless because hope is ever present. We may ask God why something is happening to us, but through experience and faith we accept our circumstances—though we usually don't understand why.

But this matter of innocent people suffering—that is something very different, and it's tough to deal with. Often the pain we feel for others is greater than the pain we feel for ourselves. Like the girl on the plane, we want to know why God didn't stop the shooter in Orlando, or why he didn't prevent the Boko Haram kidnappers or the ISIS beheaders from doing their evil deeds. Why doesn't God stop the slaughter of the innocents?

We get it. We feel what you feel. But then we have to ask ourselves another more personal question: Why doesn't God stop *us*?

Huh? Where did that come from! Well, we already introduced this idea in chapter 3, thanks to Joni Eareckson Tada: "If God being good means that he has to get rid of sin, it means he would have to get rid of sinners." You probably caught on to the stark implication of that statement, but then dismissed it. It's easy to rationalize that yes, we're sinners, but we don't crucify, behead, or enslave people. We don't harm children. We may do bad stuff, but nothing *that* bad. Consequently, we are able to direct our outrage at God because we don't like it that he hasn't gotten rid of people a lot worse than us.

When we stay on the human level, we can always find people who are worse sinners than we are. But when we compare ourselves with God, we realize that we're all sinners. As we will point out in the next chapter, the effect of evil deeds is the same—cheating on your taxes has a different effect than beheading people—but every human sins because every human is a sinner. The Bible puts it this way: "For everyone has sinned; we all fall short of God's glorious standard" (Romans 3:23 NLT). Not some of us, not most of us, but *all* of us.

QUESTIONS FOR REFLECTION AND DISCUSSION

- What do all of the horrific events mentioned in this chapter have in common? How are they different? Which ones affect you the most?
- Why is it that we can usually deal with the suffering in our lives better than we can the suffering of others?
- How would you define an "innocent" person?
- Which of these statements is more accurate: (1) "We sin because we are sinners," or (2) "We are sinners because we sin"?

There Are No Good People

In his book *Making Sense Out of Suffering*, the Catholic philosopher Peter Kreeft puts it matter-of-factly: "Why do bad things happen to good people? It is that there are no 'good people.'"[2] Or for the purposes of this chapter, there are no *innocent* people. That may seem a little harsh, but think about it. Where do sin, suffering, and death—Peter Kreeft calls these the "three evils"[3]— come from? Are they from God or from us? (We'll pause briefly for you to answer.)

Of course, all three come from us. But it's not like we didn't have an opportunity to get it right. In the beginning (as the book of Genesis starts out), God created a perfect world without sin, suffering, and death. As we have already discussed, God also created people in his image who had free wills. They had the capacity to choose to love and obey God, or to turn away and disobey God. As our representative, Adam declared his independence from God, thereby bringing the three evils into the world. Here's how a prophet, an apostle, and God himself explain it:

> All of us have become like one who is unclean, and all our righteous acts are like filthy rags; we all shrivel up like a leaf, and like the wind our sins sweep us away.
>
> Isaiah 64:6

> Therefore, just as sin entered the world through one man, and death through sin, and in this way death came to all people, because all sinned.
>
> Romans 5:12

> "From the least to the greatest, all are greedy for gain; prophets and priests alike, all practice deceit."
>
> Jeremiah 6:13

According to the prophet Isaiah, even our best efforts are like "filthy rags." He's not talking about bad people doing bad stuff. This is the effect of good people trying to do good things. Kreeft puts it this way: "Our generosity is mixed with self-interest, our passion for justice mixed with our lust for vengeance, our love for God mixed with our fear of God."[4]

The Disease and the Cure

What we don't want you to take away from this is that God won't use you because even your best efforts are subpar, or to think that someone else is so bad they are beyond God's love. In this culture of shaming through social media, we are quick to condemn and slow to forgive. Thankfully, God is just the opposite. He is slow to condemn (see John 3:17) and quick to forgive (see 1 John 1:9). God is this way because of his great love for us, but he's also this way because we are his creation, made in his image (see Genesis 1:26–27). The vilest offender is still made in the image of God. Both righteous people and despicable people (sometimes it's hard to tell the two apart) have a disease, and both need the cure.

"The two essential points of Christian doctrine are sin and salvation, the disease and the cure," writes Kreeft.[5] And it may just be that suffering is necessary for the cure. If Jesus suffered so that he could provide salvation, what makes us think we can avoid suffering in our pursuit of the cure? We're not just talking about the cure that comes when we surrender our lives to Christ and follow him. The kind of cure we have in mind is the ongoing, day-to-day experience of living faithfully as a Christian in a broken world. Jesus summed up the prescription for the cure in what is known as the Great Commandment:

> "'Love the Lord your God with all your heart and with all your soul and with all your mind.' This is the first and greatest commandment. And the second is like it: 'Love your neighbor as yourself.' All the Law and the Prophets hang on these two commandments."
>
> Matthew 22:37–40

Following the Great Commandment isn't easy. Loving God means setting aside our egos and our agendas. It means rearranging our priorities so that God and his way of doing things are our primary concern (see Matthew 6:33). It means putting the interests of others before our own. This is easier said than done, however, because following what Jesus said comes with a price. It can lead to a place of suffering. How can loving God and loving others lead to suffering? Jesus explains:

94

"If anyone would come after me, let him deny himself and take up his cross and follow me. For whoever would save his life will lose it, but whoever loses his life for my sake will find it."

Matthew 16:24–25 ESV

Notice Jesus doesn't say, "Get comfortable first and then follow me," or "Have a happy life and if you can work it in, take up your cross." He says, "Deny yourself and take up your cross." This is not trivial and it's not easy. Taking up your cross means exposing yourself to the same kind of treatment Jesus received.

"'Show me my cross' may be a statement every Christian needs to say to the world," says Mako Fujimura, referring to the eleven-year-old on Martyrs Hill. "For each follower 'to carry his own cross' means to expect persecution, betrayal, and exile from the world."[6]

QUESTIONS FOR REFLECTION AND DISCUSSION

- Peter Kreeft calls sin, suffering, and death the "three evils." Describe the differences between the three. How are they related?
- How many times a day do you judge others as worse than you? Give a couple of examples.
- Jesus makes it clear that following him is a sacrifice and can lead to suffering. Why don't pastors and churches communicate this message?

Hate What Is Evil

Taking up our cross means being willing to suffer—not just for ourselves, but for the sake of others. If you are asking, "Why did God let this happen to me?" you are asking an appropriate question, but it doesn't necessarily rise to the level of cross-taking. When you ask, "Why is God letting this happen to *them*?" and you feel the pain and the evil they are experiencing, you are taking "Love your neighbor as yourself" to heart. Even more, you are getting to a place where you have God's heart for the world, so that the things that break his heart also break yours.

The Bible tells us to "hate what is evil" (Romans 12:9). This isn't God telling us to do his job for him. When we hate what God hates, we are aligning ourselves with him. When we get angry at sin, we are, in a sense, becoming like him, which is exactly what he wants us to do.

In his book *When There Are No Easy Answers*, John Feinberg writes that evil happens to us because we live in a fallen world. This isn't resignation, but recognition. It's being aware of the reality around us, which for Feinberg is unthinkably harsh. You see, his wife has Huntington's chorea, a genetically transmitted disease that results in the death of brain cells. Symptoms are both physical and psychological.

You might think Feinberg, as a professor of biblical and systematic theology at a well-known Christian university, has come to terms with the disease that has devastated his wife and family for nearly thirty years. But it hasn't been that way. Feinberg has struggled with the problem of suffering and evil on a very personal level. He agrees with Keller that this isn't something you can process rationally. It's fundamentally an emotional issue. "My problem," writes Feinberg, "was about how in the midst of affliction I could find comfort, and how I could find it in myself to live with the God who wasn't stopping the suffering."[7] As he processed the affliction he and his wife were experiencing, Feinberg arrived at two conclusions that have helped him cope.

First, he became angry at sin. "Realizing this," he writes, "one understands that though my wife committed no specific sin after birth that brought this upon her, this has in fact happened because of her sin in Adam—though she is no more and no less responsible than the rest of us."[8] Feinberg concludes that he needed to channel his emotions through hatred—not at God, but at sin. "If we see sin from God's perspective, we need to hate it,"[9] he says, echoing Romans 12:9.

Feinberg's second epiphany is at the heart of dealing with suffering and evil, whether from your own experience or embodied in someone else's: Help yourself by helping others. In the midst of Feinberg's wife's suffering and his own despair, God gave Feinberg the opportunity to shift the focus off his problems and onto the needs of others. "For those wrestling with some affliction, as you are able, seek ways to help others," he says. "There is therapeutic value in getting your eyes off your problems."[10]

Turning from self to others when suffering is involved is not easy. For Feinberg, it took years. If you're in the midst of personal suffering, don't expect to make the transition overnight. On the other hand, if you are troubled by the suffering of others, this shift in focus can happen quickly. Consider the following example from Scripture.

Peter and the Lame Beggar

The third chapter of the New Testament book of Acts tells the story of two disciples of Jesus encountering a man who was lame from birth. Peter and John were on their way to the temple to worship when a crippled man slumped outside the entrance asked them for money. We can identify with this scene. If you live in a city, you've seen people at intersections with cardboard signs asking for help. Of course, if you're like us, your natural instinct is to avoid eye contact and hope the signal quickly turns green. Not so with Peter and the lame beggar. The Bible says, "Peter looked straight at him" (Acts 3:4). He then told him, "Silver or gold I do not have, but what I do have I give you. In the name of Jesus Christ of Nazareth, walk" (Acts 3:6–7).

We're not suggesting that you quote Peter word for word next time you pass someone in need. God isn't calling you to be a faith healer (at least we don't think he is). What he is calling you to be, however, is someone who reveals God's love and goodness in a broken world. Following the example of Peter as described in the book of Acts, here are three things we can do to accomplish this whenever the opportunity comes our way:

Peter looked straight at him. This is so hard to do, isn't it? When a suffering face looks at us, pleading for help, our tendency is to look away. But Peter showed the crippled man dignity by looking him in the eyes. He looked intently and earnestly at the man. His eyes showed compassion. An old saying goes, "The eyes are a window to the soul." That's not in the Bible, but we think the principle applies. The way we view others, the manner in which we see suffering, whether it's in someone close or very far away, reveals our heart.

"What I do have I give you." The passage in Acts tells us that the crippled man was carried daily to "the temple gate called Beautiful" (verse 2). This was a gate made out of silver and gold, so when Peter responded to the beggar's plea for help, he was referring to these precious materials. He didn't have such riches, but he was willing to give what he had. Obviously, Peter gave the beggar something far greater than silver and gold, and he did so in the name and authority of Jesus. The beggar asked Peter and John to solve a temporary problem, but Peter helped him with a much bigger problem. Oh, that we would have the eyes to see the bigger problems, and the faith to believe that God can use us to help in ways that stretch beyond our human ability.

Taking him by the right hand, he helped him up. Isn't this a beautiful phrase? The crippled man didn't know yet what had happened, but Peter physically helped him to his feet. What a marvelous picture of what God desires to do with us, and how much he wants us to help others.

You may feel overwhelmed and perhaps intimidated by the daunting task of helping people in need. Seeing a guy on the street with a cardboard sign is one thing, but helping people who are desperate and hurting beyond anything we can imagine seems beyond our feeble faith. You may feel like Mako did that day on Martyrs Hill—feeling traumatized beyond your experience. Don't let that fear keep you from doing something, and don't for a minute believe that unless you do something big, you shouldn't do anything at all. As Andy Stanley has said, "Do for one what you wish you could do for everyone."

QUESTIONS FOR REFLECTION AND DISCUSSION

- Have you ever struggled to live with a God who isn't stopping the suffering in the world? How do you deal with that?
- Explain how getting angry at sin and helping others are very much related.
- What thoughts go through your head when you see someone with a cardboard sign standing on a street corner?
- What do you do when you feel overwhelmed by all the suffering and injustice in the world?

Pig Farming in Uganda

We know of some families who felt the way Mako did, but in a very different circumstance. On a mission trip to Uganda, they were confronted by the plight of more than twenty million girls and women who are the victims of human trafficking worldwide. Tens of thousands of them are from Uganda, where the average age of entry into sexual exploitation is thirteen. These girls are sold into a life of slavery and sexual exploitation, and while the awareness of this horrific practice is growing, less than one percent of the victims are being rescued and given the aftercare services they so desperately need.

Believing they could and should do something, these families saw the need and decided to develop an ongoing, sustainable revenue source in Uganda for the benefit of the most vulnerable, while sharing the gospel and eternal hope found in Jesus Christ. In fact, their organization is known as Eternal Hope. Here's how it works:

Many of the Ugandan girls are kidnapped and sold into slavery in China, trapped with no way out. The families prayed for an opportunity to help in a significant way and came up with the idea for an enterprise in Uganda that could provide funding for the rescue and long-term aftercare for these broken girls. After doing their due diligence, they settled on a simple business model that would end up yielding big results: a commercial pig farm. Despite the fact that the average Ugandan consumes seven and a half pounds of pork annually (the highest per capita consumption in Africa), there were no commercial pig farms.

By locating their farm in a strategic tribal location outside Kampala, the capital of Uganda, the families have introduced a sustainable revenue source that is having a positive economic, social, and spiritual impact within the community. One hundred percent of the profits are dedicated to rescuing and redeeming girls trapped in a life of slavery and sexual exploitation. Following their rescue, the girls are welcomed into a loving home, where they know they are loved and cared for. They receive educational opportunities and are taught a trade so they can support themselves economically.

Each of the girls experiences healing and has hope for the first time in her life, all because the love of Jesus and a heart for those who are suffering led some people to do for a few what they can't do for all. (Discover more about the work and ministry of Eternal Hope at www.eternalhope.net.)

Suffering and the Grace of God

In this whole matter of the suffering of others, especially those who seem innocent and did nothing to deserve their plight, a question inevitably arises. If you are the sensitive type (and we hope you are), you might be wondering, "Why do they suffer and I don't?" Or if you are the one who is suffering, you could be asking, "Why am I afflicted while others seem to have it better?"

These are fair questions because they go to the heart of God's fairness, or at least that's what we think. John Feinberg, whose wife and family are the ones who are suffering, encourages us to view this through the lens of *grace* rather than *fairness*. "God isn't obligated to keep me from my trials just because he hasn't give you those afflictions," he writes. "Giving grace to you doesn't mean he has been unfair to me."[11]

The reason for this is that grace is by definition "unmerited favor." It's God giving us what we don't deserve. In a fallen world, where we are the ones who have offended a holy God by our sin, God does not *owe* grace to anyone. "I have no right to envy you when God gives you grace he has withheld from me," Feinberg continues, "because he has a right to do with grace whatever he chooses." [12]

You may be in that position, where your life is going fine. You aren't suffering like the girls in Uganda or like John Feinberg's family. Should you feel guilty that God has been so gracious for you? Absolutely not. Be thankful that you are the recipient of God's grace, and do what you can to be God's instrument of grace to others. And as you're doing so, there are two opposite attitudes you should avoid.

First, don't reject those who suffer as morally and spiritually inferior to you just because you have received grace. You did nothing to earn God's favor, so don't think for a minute that you aren't suffering because you're a better person. Second, don't feel guilty because others are suffering and you're not. Feinberg's perspective is helpful:

> If God in his sovereign wisdom chooses to give you grace, don't feel guilty as though either you or God has done something wrong. Rather, rejoice and praise him for the grace that spared you the suffering. In addition, feel compassion toward those who haven't escaped, and do whatever you can to help them bear their burdens. [13]

QUESTIONS FOR REFLECTION AND DISCUSSION

- Can you think of any other examples of enterprises, like the pig farm in Uganda, that are bringing hope to the helpless?
- How is it that God can be both gracious and fair, even though these two actions seem to be very different?
- Have you ever felt guilty for having a good life while others suffer? Have you ever been resentful when the opposite is true? How has this chapter helped you deal with these emotions?

7

Is There a Difference between the Evil in the World and the Sin in Me?

Introduction

The most often cited examples of the evil that people are capable of are the actions of the Nazi soldiers and commanders against the Jews in World War II. The Nuremberg Trials, held from 1945 to 1949, brought the horrors of the Third Reich to the public stage as witnesses told stories of the atrocities in vivid detail. Yet those reporters who came to the trials expecting to find "sadistic monsters" were disappointed. These weren't evil-looking creatures, but ordinary men "who may have been good fathers, kind to animals, even unassuming, yet who committed unspeakable crimes."[1]

One reporter in particular, Hannah Arendt, wrote of "the banality of evil." Most Nuremberg defendants never intended to be the world's most hated villains, she observed. Instead, they bought into an ideological cause and became numb to the evil they perpetuated. They suffered from a lack of empathy for their fellow human beings. On one level, their decisions to murder and maim were the results of their "career-motivated decisions."[2]

Not Like Him

In 1945, when World War II came to an end, the world was a much different place than it is today. Cars got terrible gas mileage. Television was black and white. Rock 'n' roll wasn't born yet. And people were used to hearing the word *sin*, probably because the ramifications of Nazi evil were still fresh in everyone's minds. How times have changed. We've got electric cars, color TV on our individual smartphones, and all the rock music we can handle. And the word *sin* is all but scrubbed from our vernacular.

You would be hard pressed to find a Sunday sermon about sin these days. Preachers don't like to preach about it because people don't like to hear about it. In fact, most people's knee-jerk reaction to this chapter's question—"Is there a difference between the evil in the world and the sin in me?"—is "Of course there is!"

Not only are we less likely to hear about sin these days, but we're also less likely to think of ourselves as sinful. There was a time (back in that gas-guzzling, black-and-white era) when the lines between good and evil were less blurry, but there is a newly acquired cultural resistance to the idea that we are sinful.

We are dumbfounded by the actions of the Nazis because we could never conceive of doing such things. We breathe a sigh of relief and feel good about ourselves, remembering we are not like "those Nazis." But in our pious self-assurance, we have to admit the Nazis were human beings just like us. We have to acknowledge that evil is done, not by sadistic monsters, but by ordinary people. And if we have any doubts about this, the Holy Spirit brings to mind (inconveniently) a story Jesus told, recorded in the Gospel of Luke.

> Then Jesus told this story to some who had great confidence in their own righteousness and scorned everyone else: "Two men went to the Temple to pray. One was a Pharisee, and the other was a despised tax

collector. The Pharisee stood by himself and prayed this prayer: 'I thank you, God, that I am not like other people—cheaters, sinners, adulterers. I'm certainly not like that tax collector! I fast twice a week, and I give you a tenth of my income.'

"But the tax collector stood at a distance and dared not even lift his eyes to heaven as he prayed. Instead, he beat his chest in sorrow, saying, 'O God, be merciful to me, for I am a sinner.' I tell you, this sinner, not the Pharisee, returned home justified before God. For those who exalt themselves will be humbled, and those who humble themselves will be exalted."

Luke 18:9–14 NLT

This story vanquishes our feelings of moral superiority as we easily catch Jesus' drift. We're not supposed to look down our noses at other "sinners," thinking we're better. We know God doesn't want us playing judge and jury.

What gets our goat is Jesus' leveling of the playing field. Is he saying these men's sins are the same? Weren't first-century Pharisees better people than tax collectors, crooks who robbed their fellow Jews while working for the occupying Roman army? Aren't religious men morally superior to cheaters, thieves, and traitors? Aren't we better than those Nazi criminals? We're not perfect, that's for sure. But we really *aren't* like some other people, right?

QUESTIONS FOR REFLECTION AND DISCUSSION

- What was your initial reaction to this chapter's opening story?
- How does Jesus' parable hit you?
- Why do you think it's difficult for people to talk about sin?

Is All Sin the Same?

There's a common phrase among some churchgoers: "Sin is sin." At first blush, it's intuitive. If something is wrong, it's wrong. But one glance at the world's nastiness, and it's obvious that all sins are *not* the same. Facing crimes like rape, armed robbery, torture, child abuse, and murder makes the phrase "Sin is sin" feel trite and dismissive.

Cornelius Plantinga Jr. agrees. Plantinga wrote one of our favorite books about sin (can one really have a favorite book about sin?). In *Not the Way It's Supposed to Be*, he says this:

> All sin is equally wrong, but not all sin is equally bad. Acts are either right or wrong, either consonant with God's will or not. But among good acts some are better than others, and among wrong acts some worse than others. Christians believe that thinking deliciously about adultery is just as wrong as committing it. . . . But Christians also know that adultery in one's heart damages others less, at least for the short term, than does adultery in a motel room.[3]

Plantinga is right. All sin is not the same. Dealing insults and gossiping behind someone's back is sinful, but it's a far cry from burning their house down. There are sins that hurt more deeply and more immediately than others. But was Jesus truly implying that "sin is sin"? Are repentant extortionist tax collectors more justified before God than the prideful religious leader? The answer is yes . . . and no. Even though different sins result in varying degrees of felt pain, when all is said and done, they share the same root. And that root is buried deep within all of us.

What Is Sin?

In our book *Answering the Toughest Questions About Heaven and Hell*, we cite Plantinga's definition for sin. It will again prove helpful. Plantinga calls sin the "vandalism of *shalom*." *Shalom* is a Hebrew word in the Old Testament, and Plantinga captures well its rich, and important, definition.

> The webbing together of God, humans, and all creation in justice, fulfillment, and delight is what the Hebrew prophets called *shalom*. We call it peace, but it means far more than mere peace of mind or

a cease-fire between enemies. In the Bible, *shalom* means universal flourishing, wholeness, and delight—a rich state of affairs in which natural needs are satisfied and natural gifts fruitfully employed, a state of affairs that inspires joyful wonder as its Creator and Savior opens doors and welcomes the creatures in whom he delights. *Shalom*, in other words, is the way things ought to be.[4]

Seminary professor Marguerite Shuster defines sin simply. She says sin is the infringement on the two primary imperatives from God: "Love the Lord your God with all your heart and with all your soul and with all your mind" and "Love your neighbor as yourself" (Matthew 22:37, 39).[5]

Both theologians agree that God designed the world with *shalom*, but that perfect picture was defiled and broken by sin: the refusal to do what is in God's top two commands.

If that is sin, what is evil? In her book *The Fall and Sin*, Shuster writes, "Sin is, first and most basically, an evil."[6]

Our culture cringes at this idea. We don't like to think we're sinners, much less evil. We reduce sin to "overindulgence," and we self-soothe by thinking only the likes of bin Laden and Stalin, ISIS and Nazis, Jeffrey Dahmer and Charles Manson are evil. But the Bible takes a different tack.

There are over sixty different words in Hebrew and Greek (the Bible's original languages) that describe sin. Each describes a breach of God's will. "Evil" and "evil desires" are part of that list.[7] A single English word, *sin*, can't capture it all, but according to God's Word, all sin is evil.

> **QUESTIONS FOR REFLECTION AND DISCUSSION**
> - Do you find yourself categorizing sins in your life or in others' lives? How do you group them?
> - How would you have defined sin before? Why did you define it that way?
> - What do you think about *shalom*? What about sin as a violation of it?

All of Us

It's a bummer, but we get this nagging feeling that the apostle Paul is right. In Romans 3:23 he wrote, "For everyone has sinned; we all fall short of God's glorious standard" (NLT). That's all of us. And unless you're ready for a reality check, don't bother reading Jesus' most famous sermon, called the Sermon on the Mount, captured in Matthew 5–7. In it, Jesus raises—not lowers—the bar for perfection. Jesus doesn't identify how sinful we are because he's a judgmental finger-pointer, but because he loves us deeply. He wants to truth-fully diagnose our sin disease so that he can lead us to the cure. The sermon starts with the revelation that God, in Christ, doles out gen-erous helpings of his undeserved love and favor. Jesus then teaches that life is not only about how we act, but also about how we think.

- Jesus confirmed murder is wrong, but he also included slaying others with our contempt in the sin category (see Matthew 5:21–22).
- Sex with someone other than your spouse is still sinful, Jesus taught, but so is imagining it (see 5:27–30).
- It's sin to break our promises. But we don't need to hide behind vague oaths. Rather, our simple yes or no should suffice (see 5:33–37).
- Other portions of the sermon instruct Jesus' followers to *think* differently about revenge (see 5:38–42), their enemies (see 5:43–48), their spiritual acts (see 6:18), and what con-sumes their thoughts and fears (see 6:25–34).

Jesus knows (because he's God, after all) that sin is more than skin deep. Sin's cancer infects and multiplies in our minds, not just our bodies.

So it's official. We are all sinners. This is difficult to face, but we instinctively know it's true. We might not have killed anybody, but we've more than once wished someone was a goner. We've never cheated on our wives with our bodies, but our minds are guilty.

We've never taken the law into our own hands, but we regularly judge others for what we deem sinful.

"Everyone knows about temptations to do wrong, and everyone knows something about succumbing."[8] At least we're not alone. There is some comfort in that.

Say It Ain't So

Have you ever so deeply wanted something to be true that you refused to see it wasn't? The hit reality TV show *American Idol* is a classic example. *American Idol* took regular folks who could sing and turned them into pop stars. In the auditions, thousands of hopeful musicians were cut. Some were average singers. Others were absolutely terrible (and Simon Cowell loved to tell them so). One would think that someone—anyone—would have discouraged those with horrendous pipes from singing on national television. But they didn't. The performers (and their mothers) so deeply believed they could be famous singers that they refused to face the music (pun intended).

This makes for embarrassingly good entertainment, but we all know it's a terrible way to live. Yet most of us do it. We justify our behavior, refusing to believe what is real. We believe more money will satisfy us. But it can't. We believe our kids are more special than anyone else's. But they aren't. We desperately want to believe all religions teach the same thing in pursuit of the same God. But they don't.

This phenomenon applies to sin, too. We so deeply desire for sin to be innocuous that we justify our behavior and thoughts and ignore the results. It's no big deal. It doesn't hurt anyone. God will look the other way. We repeat these statements because we really, *really* want them to be true. But as a wise redneck once said, "You can wish in one hand and spit in the other, and see which one fills up faster."

The reality is that sin is a *huge* deal. It *always* hurts people. And our good God *cannot* look the other way. Sin is a killer, and it's what is killing us. And God is not content to let that be.

Perversion, pollution, disintegration

Cornelius Plantinga astutely points out that sin kills in three distinct ways. It perverts, pollutes, and disintegrates.

Perversion is the repurposing of our "loyalty, energy, and desire away from God and God's project in the world."[9] We use money for greedy purposes instead of generous ones. We leverage relationships for power and control instead of loving, serving, and sacrificing for each other. We think God's gracious gifts are entitlements, and we obsess over them accordingly. This is perversion of God's will and design.

The second way sin kills is *pollution*. Plantinga puts it like this: "To pollute is to weaken a particular whole entity, such as a sound relationship, by introducing into it a foreign element. . . . The image of pollution suggests bringing together what ought to be kept apart."[10] Perversion and pollution go hand in hand. For instance, when God's design for sex is perverted, it pollutes marriages and families. When religion is perverted by power, it pollutes churches, countries, and souls.

Disintegration is the third way sin kills. If pollution kills by addition, then disintegration kills by division. Idolatry (putting anything before God) divides our loyalties, corrupting our relationship with God and others. We cannot be fully devoted to two things (see Luke 16:13). The beauty of what the Bible teaches is that full devotion placed in God allows everything else to fall into its proper order and place (see Matthew 6:33; 22:37–40).

Sin perverts, pollutes, and disintegrates, and under its influence life and relationships weaken, break, crumble, and dissolve.

QUESTIONS FOR REFLECTION AND DISCUSSION

- How do you react to Jesus' teaching about sinful action and thought?
- How do you see people justifying their sin? How do you justify your sin?

- Have you ever wanted to believe something that wasn't true? What was it?
- How does seeing the truth about sin—even when difficult—help?

The Slippery Slope

Mesillat Yesharim, a text on ethics written by the influential eighteenth-century rabbi Moshe Chaim Luzzatto, contains this saying about the total corruption of sin: "If a man is allured by the things of this world and is estranged from his Creator, it is not he alone who is corrupted, but the whole world is corrupted with him."[11]

It's a compelling quote, and an argument the Bible makes clearly and forthrightly. Our sin not only makes us dirty before God, but drags the whole world through the mud. Rabbi Luzzatto boldly wrote the truth: Sin corrupts our souls, breaks our relationship with God and others, and simultaneously corrupts the world.

But is this really true? Does our disobedience to God add more cracks to a shattered world? Is that even *possible*? It's easy to see how the big sins (e.g., adultery, robbing banks, hurting kids, shooting somebody) pervert, pollute, and disintegrate. That's nasty stuff. But if we're guilty of nothing on that wicked list, how are we contributing to evil? At first it's difficult to see how our "little" sins corrupt our world. But dig a little deeper with us, and you'll see it's not only true, but readily apparent.

Sin begets sin

The tricky thing about sin is that it refuses to go solo. Sin begets sin. Like fungus, it grows in the dark, multiplying in the absence of light. Once again, Plantinga describes it well:

Sin is "an evil tree" that yields "corrupt fruit." Youngsters eventually discover what the wise have known for millennia: people rarely commit single sins. . . . Sins and products of sin keep on

111

replicating and bunching together like clusters of grapes on the vine. The clusters show up in individual persons but also in groups (in family systems, for instance) and in the places where groups and individuals meet. Hence the corruption of persons, of communities, and of whole cultures.[12]

True-to-life examples of this phenomenon abound.

- Plantinga describes a high school girl who "watches television when she should be studying and snaps at a parent who gestures toward her unopened books. The next afternoon she cheats on the first of her semester exams. Then, feeling irritable, she gets drunk with her friends, gossips more maliciously than usual about an acquaintance they all dislike, and—blood alcohol level still rising—aggressively drives her mother's car home. Indeed, she drives it part way through the end of the garage. Afterward she doesn't feel like studying."[13]

- A businessman makes a shady deal in lean times and turns a profit. Things look up. Another lie is told, another income bump produced. Soon lies and profits, cutting corners, and telling half-truths are linked in regular business. Before long he wonders why clients cheat him and his kids don't tell the truth.

- A woman not in love marries to have children. She pours her life into her kids but not her husband. She creates an imaginary competition between herself and other moms, and her love for her children becomes performance based. She is fulfilled and brags when they win, is disappointed and scolds when they lose. Decades later they avoid her and her overprotective meddling, yet find burned deep inside themselves an almost irresistible urge to control and alienate *their* children and spouses.

- A pastor's job becomes his identity. He replaces his family with "the family of God" through subtle shifts in time and priority. His family grows bitter, his congregation more demanding. Ironically, he derives his value from an ever-sinking approval rating, and in his loneliness and self-pity he drinks more and more to cope.

Are any of these folks serial killers or child pornographers? No. But does their sin multiply, almost without their knowing, causing negative impact all around them? Certainly. Does it destroy like a terrorist's bomb? Perhaps not as quickly or surprisingly, but just because it doesn't make the evening news doesn't mean it isn't evil and lives aren't affected.

Our tendency to think of sin as solely a personal issue prevents us from seeing the truth. As sin begets sin in individuals, corruption grows in families, organizations, communities, and countries. This multiplication is particularly true when sin invades the lives of influential people.

At a friend's birthday party I (Chris) sat next to a young woman who had recently met two famous men (a politician and an entertainer). Though they were vastly different, she said, both had intoxicating charisma. She commented, "I understand why they are able to sleep with so many women." I then overheard her whisper to a girlfriend, "Married or not, I don't think I could resist sleeping with them, too, if only they asked!"

When people of prestige cheat, steal, lie, commit adultery, or abuse their power, they unwittingly encourage impressionable fans—like this young woman—to do the same. One by one, culture is changed.

Corrupt government leaders hoard resources, create dire poverty, and control others through violence. As sin's treachery trickles down, their country's destitute are tempted toward violence and thievery to survive. The poorest of poor sell their children for food, fueling a slave industry that corrupts lives of slave owners and slaves. The cycle is vicious.

Cutthroat businesspeople influence employees toward disrespect and selfishness. Gossiping, judgmental parents shape hateful kids. Prejudiced journalists fuel inequality. Lazy teachers and administrators create careless students. Abusive clergy create violent fanatics.

The examples are legion. Sin begets sin, corruption corrupts, and more than just the sinner's soul is spoiled.

"Indeed," Plantinga thoughtfully and accurately summarizes, "like cancer, sin kills *because* it reproduces."[14]

QUESTIONS FOR REFLECTION AND DISCUSSION

- Have you ever felt like your sin has been a slippery slope to more sin? Why or why not?
- What do you think about the idea that entire cultures are corrupted by the multiplication of the sins of individuals?
- How do you think the multiplication of sin is ultimately stopped?

The Redemption of Paul (and Us!)

Let's summarize (as depressing as that might be). Sin is any and all disobedience to God. Sin is evil, evil is sin. We all sin by thought and action. And sin has a nasty habit of reproducing and corrupting God's world, violating *shalom*.

It's a bummer, and we hate to report it, but it's the truth. However, it's not the *whole* truth. In fact, in response to all this bad news, there is good news. Very good news. But the only way to fully grasp and reap the benefits of the good news is to hear and know the bad news. Just as in the rest of life, the first step to fixing a problem is to admit there is a problem. And sin is definitely a problem. We've outlined that well here, so let's get on with the good news!

Few people have articulated it as thoroughly as the apostle Paul, one of the first Christian missionaries. And part of what makes his description of God's good news so rich is that this saint knew he was no saint. *The Message* Bible captures well how Paul described his own sin-bent soul.

> I'm full of myself—after all, I've spent a long time in sin's prison. What I don't understand about myself is that I decide one way, but then I act another, doing things I absolutely despise. . . . I realize

that I don't have what it takes. I can will it, but I can't *do* it. I decide to do good, but I don't *really* do it; I decide not to do bad, but then I do it anyway. My decisions, such as they are, don't result in actions. Something has gone wrong deep within me and gets the better of me every time.

It happens so regularly that it's predictable. The moment I decide to do good, sin is there to trip me up. I truly delight in God's commands, but it's pretty obvious that not all of me joins in that delight. Parts of me covertly rebel, and just when I least expect it, they take charge.

I've tried everything and nothing helps. I'm at the end of my rope. Is there no one who can do anything for me?

Romans 7:14–24 THE MESSAGE

Paul knew he was defeated. *Even* Paul—someone virtually every Christian on the planet admires—came face-to-face with his sin and its impact on him and the world. Paul also came face-to-face with the one and only cure for sin. Paul met the living Christ and found the answer to his desperate question.

The answer, thank God, is that Jesus Christ can and does. He acted to set things right in this life of contradictions where I want to serve God with all my heart and mind, but am pulled by the influence of sin to do something totally different.

With the arrival of Jesus, the Messiah, that fateful dilemma is resolved. Those who enter into Christ's being-here-for-us no longer have to live under a continuous, low-lying black cloud. A new power is in operation. The Spirit of life in Christ, like a strong wind, has magnificently cleared the air, freeing you from a fated lifetime of brutal tyranny at the hands of sin and death.

God . . . didn't deal with the problem as something remote and unimportant. In his Son, Jesus, he personally took on the human condition, entered the disordered mess of struggling humanity in order to set it right once and for all. . . . Instead of redoubling our own efforts, simply embrace what the Spirit is doing in us.

Those who trust God's action in them find that God's Spirit is in them—living and breathing God! . . . For you who welcome him, in whom he dwells—even though you still experience all the limitations of sin—you yourself experience life on God's terms. . . . When God lives and breathes in you (and he does, as surely as he did in Jesus), you are delivered from that dead life. . . .

I'm absolutely convinced that nothing—nothing living or dead, angelic or demonic, today or tomorrow, high or low, thinkable or unthinkable—absolutely nothing can get between us and God's love because of the way that Jesus our Master has embraced us.

Romans 7:25; 8:1–5, 10–11, 38–39 THE MESSAGE

The key to hope in Jesus despite being broken by sin is found in these two truths: First, the evil in the world is the result of sin in us. But second, God is *so* much bigger and more powerful than sin. To receive God's power to fight sin and to live eternally with him despite it, all we must do is recognize our sinfulness, thank him and accept his gift of love in Jesus, and invite him to live, by his Spirit, in us from this moment on. And with that, the power of God that Jesus experienced in his life, death, resurrection, and ascension is available to us to fight sin in us and in the world until his promised return.

QUESTIONS FOR REFLECTION AND DISCUSSION

- Summarize in two or three sentences Paul's argument in Romans 7. What phrases did you notice? What is the single message that stands out to you the most?

- What if you had the first part of this section (Romans 7:14–24) but not the rest of it? How would you feel?

- In what ways does the second part of the Romans passage outline the good news message of Jesus Christ?

8

What's the Point
of Suffering?

Introduction

If you want to write a story filled with suspense, don't give away the ending on the first page. Yet that's exactly what Paul Kalanithi does in his bestselling book, *When Breath Becomes Air*. There's no use trying to hide it, so we're also going to give you the ending: Paul dies.

Now, even though you know how Paul's story ends, get the book. This is one of the most moving true stories you will ever read, and it goes directly to the heart of what we're going to talk about in this chapter: What's the point of suffering?

Dr. Paul Kalanithi was a gifted neurosurgeon (and a brilliant writer, by the way). On the verge of completing a decade of school and training that included medical school, residency, and an appointment at Stanford, Paul was also married to the love of his life with plans to start a family. Then came the symptoms and the diagnosis: Paul had stage 4 lung cancer.

With access to skilled doctors, along with his own deep understanding of the treatment options, Paul fought valiantly. But it wasn't surviving physically that mattered most to him. As his decline quickened, he had another purpose in mind—to help people understand death and face their mortality. As his wife, Lucy Kalanithi, writes in the book's epilogue, "He wanted to help people understand death and face their mortality. Dying in one's fourth decade is unusual now, but *dying* is not."[1]

In an email to a friend, Paul explained what he was aiming for in his writing. "Not the sensationalism of dying, and not exhortation to gather rose buds, but: Here's what lies up ahead on the road." Paul died while working on his book. Throughout his life, he wrestled "with the question of how to live a meaningful life, and his book explains that essential territory."[2]

The End Is Better Than the Beginning

"Words have a longevity I do not."[3] Is this what drove Paul to write? It would seem that's the case, and he wouldn't be the first. Twenty centuries before Paul wrote *When Breath Becomes Air*, a wise teacher, possibly King Solomon, wrote these words:

> It is better to go to a house of mourning than to go to a house of feasting, for death is the destiny of everyone; the living should take this to heart.
>
> Ecclesiastes 7:2

A few verses later, the teacher writes, "The end of the matter is better than its beginning" (Ecclesiastes 7:8). If you interpret this to mean that the day of a person's death is better than the day of his birth, you are reading it right. Too pessimistic? We admit it's a bit on the dark side, but only if you really are a pessimist. If you're a Christian and you truly believe the end of this life on earth is but a portal to the afterlife Jesus promised us (see John 14:1–4), then the day you die will beat the day you were born. Hands down.

"That is the day of ultimate triumph for the Christian in this world," writes R. C. Sproul in his classic book *Surprised by Suffering*, "and yet it is a day we fear and a day we postpone as long as we possibly can because we don't *really* believe that the day of our death is better than the day of our birth."[4]

How We Get Suffering Wrong

What applies to death also applies to suffering. We fear it and consequently do all we can to avoid or postpone it because we don't really believe suffering can be beneficial. Like so many things in life, we fear suffering because we don't understand it. In fact, we think there are a couple of ways we get suffering wrong.

We think God wants us to be happy all the time

This mistaken notion is prevalent in the church today (more about this in chapter 9). A problem-free life is the goal of many Christians. They thank God when things are going well but question God's goodness when bad things happen. But that's just bad theology. God doesn't work that way. This is what the teacher says about good and bad times:

> When times are good, be happy; but when times are bad, consider this: God has made the one as well as the other. Therefore, no one can discover anything about their future.
>
> Ecclesiastes 7:14

God is sovereign in all things, as much in our suffering as he is in our prosperity. Job, the poster boy for suffering in the Bible, puts it this way:

> "Naked I came from my mother's womb, and naked I will depart. The Lord gave and the Lord has taken away; may the name of the Lord be praised."
>
> Job 1:21

119

There are two extreme views we could take, and both distort a correct view of suffering. One is to think that God wants us to suffer, and therefore prevents us from being happy. The other is to believe God only wants us to be happy. A balanced view is to see God's sovereign rule in both the suffering and the joy we experience. As the Puritan preacher Jeremiah Burroughs wrote, "Grace gives a man an eye to see the love of God in every affliction as well as in prosperity."[5]

We think suffering is senseless

Whenever something horrible happens in the world, you often see it described as a "senseless tragedy." According to Sproul,

> The idea of a "senseless tragedy" represents a worldview that is completely incompatible with Christian thought, because it assumes that something happens without a purpose or a meaning. But if God is God and if God is a God of providence and if God is sovereign, then nothing ever happens that is senseless in the final analysis.[6]

There's nothing wrong with asking God *why* when confronted with a tragedy, whether it's in our own lives or in the life of someone else. But we shouldn't be upset when the answer doesn't come as quickly as we want. In fact, God rarely reveals the benefits to our suffering early in the journey we are on. Sometimes we never know the reason. In other circumstances, we understand at just the right moment. This happened to the Old Testament character of Joseph, who was sold into slavery by his jealous brothers, later to be thrown in prison because his master's wife falsely accused him of making advances at her.

Joseph suffered for years at the hands of his oppressors before being elevated to the second most powerful position in all of Egypt. It was only after seeing the big picture from God's perspective that he was able to tell his brothers, "You intended to harm me, but God intended it for good to accomplish what is now being done, the saving of many lives" (Genesis 50:20).

The truth is, we just don't know why God allows tragic things to happen. But we can be sure the tragedies aren't senseless. There is a reason why God allows each one.

In fact, a close reading of Romans 8:28 tells us that God works out everything—the good and the bad—for our good. "The bottom-line assumption for anyone who believes in the God of providence is that ultimately there are no tragedies," writes Sproul. "God has promised that all things that happen—all pain, all suffering, all tragedies—are but for a moment, and that He works in and through these events for the good of those who love him."[7]

QUESTIONS FOR REFLECTION AND DISCUSSION

- *When Breath Becomes Air* has become a national bestseller. Why do you think people are drawn to it?
- List at least two other applications for this statement in Ecclesiastes: "The end of the matter is better than the beginning."
- Where did the idea of "senseless tragedy" come from? How does this concept feed into our natural inclination to blame God for suffering and evil?
- Describe a time when you were going through something that made no sense until you saw the big picture.

Power in Weakness

We've been talking in this book about paradoxes in the Christian life. Among the best known is the one found in this little phrase from the apostle Paul: "For when I am weak, then I am strong" (2 Corinthians 12:10). To the general population, this makes no sense. Our culture is built on strength, power, and achievement. If you show weakness, especially to an opponent, you might as well admit defeat.

Even the church and Christians have a hard time with this concept of weakness and strength. Oh, we may say we agree, but when push comes to shove, and we feel threatened by the culture or—God forbid—the courts, we tend to do all we can to preserve our "religious rights" from being trampled. Showing weakness in the face of opposition, whether cultural or political, is not accepted.

Yet if we look at the full context of Paul's little phrase, we see that he isn't saying, "Weakness helps me get stronger." He's saying, "My strength is found in my weakness." Examples of "weakness helps me get stronger" are everywhere. Here are three we found after a quick Google search of the phrase "weakness and strength":

> All the adversity I've had in my life, all my troubles and obstacles, have strengthened me.
>
> Walt Disney

> When you go through hardships and decide not to surrender, that is strength.
>
> Arnold Schwarzenegger

> I like criticism. It makes you strong!
>
> LeBron James

Are Walt, Arnold, and LeBron in agreement with the apostle Paul? On the surface, it would seem so. Just like Paul's phrase, all three quotes start with some form of the word *weakness* and end with some form of the word *strong*. But look closer. Walt, Arnold, and LeBron describe their weaknesses as things that happen to you: *adversity, hardship, criticism.* These are all qualities linked to other circumstances or other people. The goal is to overcome them and, in doing so, gain strength.

By contrast, Paul's phrase starts with himself: "When I am weak." It is not Paul's intention to overcome his weakness in order to gain strength. Paul says his strength is actually found in his weakness. He's acutely aware of those things that have made him weak. For starters, he was given a thorn in his flesh (see 2 Corinthians 12:7). Paul doesn't tell us what this is, but it was in some way debilitating, because three times he asked God to remove it (see 12:8). But the Lord says no to Paul, telling him, "My grace is sufficient for you, for my power is made perfect in weakness" (12:9a).

Paul is not gaining strength by overcoming challenging obstacles, like Walt, Arnold, and LeBron describe. It's the Lord who is strong. Paul is still weak. In fact, Paul's weakness becomes something he can boast about "so that Christ's power may rest on me" (12:9b). He concludes his reflection on Christ's power in his weakness with these words:

> For the sake of Christ, then, I am content with weaknesses, insults, hardships, persecutions, and calamities. For when I am weak, then I am strong.
>
> 2 Corinthians 12:10 ESV

Walt, Arnold, and LeBron *overcame* their insults, hardships, persecutions, and calamities. Paul is *content* with his. Can you say the same?

- If someone *insulted* you and your beliefs, would you be content to stay silent, or would you respond defensively?
- If you went through a *hardship*, would you trust God and be content, or would you fight your way out so you wouldn't have to suffer?
- If you were *persecuted*, would you fight back, or would you be content to be treated unfairly?
- If you went through a *calamity*, would you be content to endure, or would you use every resource at your command to make things right?

These are tough questions to answer. None of us likes to admit weakness. None of us wants to be content in our suffering. Yet that is exactly what Paul is suggesting here. Our tendency is to imitate Walt, Arnold, and LeBron. We'll take the insults, hardships, persecutions, and calamities, but we reserve the right to fight back or claw our way out—with God's help, of course. But that isn't what

God is suggesting. He's not telling us, "I will be glorified when you are victorious over your weakness and your suffering." He is saying, "I will be glorified in your weakness and your suffering."

The Purpose of Weakness and Suffering

John Piper provides three helpful reasons or purposes for weakness and suffering based on Paul's reflection on his own experience.

1. *It's okay to pray for relief when you are suffering.* "God does not delight in your suffering. Satan does and must be resisted."
2. *Your humility is more important to God than your comfort.* "Humility is more important than freedom from pain." Consequently, we will totally rely on God's grace rather than on our own strength.
3. *God's purpose in our weakness is to call attention to the grace and power of his Son.* "God's design is to make you a showcase for Jesus' power," not by eliminating our weakness and suffering, "but by giving strength to endure and even rejoice in tribulation."[8]

When Persecution Backfires

The Bible is full of stories of God's people suffering because of severe opposition, only to see God work through their weaknesses

124

to accomplish his purposes. The story of the early church as told in the book of Acts is a vivid example. As the good news of the death and resurrection of Jesus Christ spread, persecution increased, scattering "God's elect" throughout the ancient Near East. In yet another one of God's paradoxes, the more intense the persecution, the more the church grew.

We don't have to look back in history to find examples of God's strength displayed in the suffering of God's people. These stories are being lived out today. David Yeghnazar was born in Iran and has the perspective of seeing firsthand what God is doing through the weakness of Muslim-born people who have become Christians. Remarkably, because of insults, hardships, persecution, and calamities, more Iranians have given their lives to Christ in the last forty years than in the previous fourteen centuries.

Yeghnazar reports that everything the state has done with the goal of destroying the Christian church has backfired. Authorities have banned and even burned the Bible, yet Iranians are hungry for God's Word like never before. In the place of churches closed by the government are countless underground house churches. Even though eight pastors have been martyred since 1980, many more have taken their place. In fact, rather than being discouraged from following Christ, persecuted Christians are attracting people to him. These people ask, "Who is this Jesus that people are so willing to suffer for?"[9]

Notice what you *don't* see in this report. The Christians in Iran didn't pray for God to remove the persecution. They didn't stage a coup and revolt against government persecution. They haven't even tried to grow strong in their weakness. Instead, these Christians have invited Jesus into their suffering and watched as his power is being displayed in their weakness. They know firsthand what Paul wrote in his letter to the church in Rome:

> Therefore, since we have been justified through faith, we have peace with God through our Lord Jesus Christ, through whom we have gained access by faith into this grace in which we now stand. And

we boast in the hope of the glory of God. Not only so, but we also glory in our sufferings, because we know that suffering produces perseverance.

Romans 5:1–3

"Suffering has not destroyed the church in Iran," writes Yegh-nazar. "Rather, suffering has deepened its dependence on God, which in turn has increased its endurance, character, and hope."[10]

QUESTIONS FOR REFLECTION AND DISCUSSION

- Is it possible for God to be glorified in our strength, not just our weakness? Why or why not?
- Using the example of Christians in Iran, explain how suffering produces perseverance.
- Give your impressions of the church in America. Is it ready for persecution?

What's the Point of Suffering?

It's one thing to see God work in nations and the church. What about in your own life? You may agree that Paul's statement "When I am weak, then I am strong" is true conceptually. But what happens when you're going through a profound loss? What if your spouse has stage 4 cancer like Dr. Kalanithi? What if you live in Haiti and an earthquake or a hurricane has taken everything from you?

We want to offer five points, or purposes, of suffering that you can apply personally. Read these, think about them, talk about them. This isn't an exhaustive list, but it's a good place to start.

Point #1: Suffering can bring joy

We're not talking about a phony happiness where everything is beautiful after a deep loss. This is a joy that comes in the form of contentment in your circumstances, no matter how bleak. It's a joy based on the love and mercy of God, not on our feelings. Remember our friend Habakkuk? At the end of his book, he is waiting for the Babylonians, whose invasion is imminent. Watch how the prophet's thoughts progress from the stark reality of his situation to joy:

> I heard and my heart pounded,
>   my lips quivered at the sound;
> decay crept into my bones,
>   and my legs trembled.
> Yet I will wait patiently for the day of calamity
>   to come on the nation invading us.
> Though the fig tree does not bud
>   and there are no grapes on the vines,
> though the olive crop fails
>   and the fields produce no food,
> though there are no sheep in the pen
>   and no cattle in the stalls,
> yet I will rejoice in the Lord,
>   I will be joyful in God my Savior.
>
> Habakkuk 3:16–18

How can the prophet be joyful at a horrible time like this? As one who has been confronted with God's love and mercy, Habakkuk is a living affirmation of God's statement "The righteous person will live by his faithfulness" (Habakkuk 2:4). He is trusting God's providence no matter what the circumstances. Even if he loses everything, he will be joyful in God his Savior. We're not saying you need to jump to this place overnight. It might take time. But when you do, you will be like the person described by James in his letter to persecuted Christians:

> Consider it pure joy, my brothers and sisters, whenever you face trials of many kinds, because you know that the testing of your faith produces perseverance. Let perseverance finish its work so that you may be mature and complete, not lacking anything.
>
> James 1:2–4

Point #2: Suffering can lead to love and kindness

In his essay "What Suffering Does," *New York Times* columnist David Brooks writes, "Happiness wants you to think about maximizing your benefits. Difficulty and suffering send you on a different course." A big point of that difference, observes Brooks, is "trying to redeem something bad by turning it into something sacred."[11] That's what Dr. Kalanithi did through his book. Nancy Guthrie, who lost two children to a rare genetic disorder, channeled her grief into speaking and writing for the benefit of those who are hurting. The title of one of her most-read books speaks volumes about the way she helps people who are hurting: *What Grieving People Wish You Knew About What Really Helps (and What Really Hurts)*.

We can think of many more examples. So can you. The point is that suffering can lead you to give more of yourself. "Recovering from suffering is not like recovering from a disease," writes Brooks. "Many people don't come out healed; they come out different. They crash through the logic of individual utility and behave paradoxically."[12]

You can add another paradox to our growing list: Those who suffer are best equipped to serve.

Point #3: Suffering can lead to God

We had never heard of Landry Fields, a professional basketball player who was a starter for the New York Knicks and the Toronto Raptors. (We aren't exactly the most dedicated sports fans in the world, so Landry's anonymity to us has no relationship to his athletic ability.) But after reading his essay, "Injury Interrupted My Idolatry," we became raving fans because of what he taught us about suffering.

Fields's professional basketball career was going along just fine until a triple threat of injuries to his elbow, hand, and hip took him out of the game and his career. By his own admission, Fields had never struggled to believe in God, but like many people, that's as far as it went. "I didn't need to trust God, because I already trusted another god, the NBA."[13] Thus, his injuries interrupted his idolatry. In its place, God gave him true faith.

> Suffering is the hook that God uses to bring us back to himself, collapsed and tired from slaving for sin. . . . I knew God existed and disapproved of the life I was living (overindulging in alcohol and sexual promiscuity), but I preached a gospel of cheap grace to make myself feel better. With the injuries, God exposed that I was relying on something other than grace painted to look like grace— a cheap grace that was as useful for my suffering as a cardboard cutout of Jesus.[14]

Maybe this has happened to you. Perhaps God has made life harder for you than you ever would have thought possible. Are you choosing to blame God, or do you see a purpose in your suffering, namely that God is trying to draw you to himself? That's what Landry Fields saw.

"I'm thankful for my injured elbow, hand, and hip, because they make me depend on God in a way that I never would have without them."[15]

C. S. Lewis saw it, too. At the beginning of his grief, he felt God had slammed the door in his face. But as he invited God into his suffering, his perspective changed. "Turned to God, my mind no longer meets that locked door."[16]

Point #4: Suffering helps us identify with Jesus

In his two letters, the apostle Peter writes a lot about suffering. He gives instructions for holy living to the scattered Christians who were suffering persecution. At the center of his advice is this explanation for what suffering does for the Christian:

> Dear friends, do not be surprised at the fiery ordeal that has come on you to test you, as though something strange were happening to you. But rejoice inasmuch as you participate in the sufferings of Christ, so that you may be overjoyed when his glory is revealed. If

you are insulted because of the name of Christ, you are blessed, for the Spirit of glory and of God rests on you.

1 Peter 4:12–14

Of all the benefits or purposes of suffering, this is the highest, for there is no higher calling than to identify with Jesus. "If you suffer as a Christian, do not be ashamed, but praise God that you bear that name" (1 Peter 4:16). God's greatest desire for us is that we be conformed to the image of his Son. If it were left to us in our prosperity, we might never get there. So he uses adversity to turn us to Jesus from our idols and our sin.

Now can you see how it's possible to be joyful in your trials? If they help you become more like Jesus, there is no greater joy.

Point #5: Suffering teaches us how to forgive

If we're going to be more like Jesus, we need to learn true forgiveness. Not the empty kind of forgiveness people offer today: "I'm sorry if anyone was offended by my actions." That's not at all what Jesus has in mind. As Bryan Loritts writes in his book *Saving the Saved*, "Jesus . . . offers no loopholes on forgiveness."[17] In his exchange with Peter, Jesus teaches him about forgiveness in a way that probably shocked him and should startle us today.

A servant in Jesus' story owed his master an insane amount of money—more than he could pay back in twenty lifetimes. The master was about to sell the man, his family, and all that he owned to pay the debt. The servant begged for mercy—in effect he asked for forgiveness of his debt—and the master canceled the debt and "let him go" (Matthew 18:27).

That's what forgiveness is. It's "letting go" of our hurts, our anger, and our bitterness over our situation. It's not easy to forgive because forgiveness itself hurts. As Tim Keller points out, forgiveness is a kind of suffering.[18] We want revenge, payback, recompense. Forgiveness lets go of all of that. At the same time, forgiveness is freeing. The servant in Jesus' story was forgiven his massive debt, but when he refused to forgive the debt of someone who owed him a fraction of the amount he owed, his master became irate and threw him in prison until he could pay his debt. "It's crazy," writes Loritts, "but when you and I refuse to forgive, we, like this servant, are not free; we end up in jail—held captive by our own unforgiveness."[19]

Father, Forgive Them

The greatest example of forgiveness is the forgiveness Jesus gave to those who were putting him to death. In effect, when he forgave them, he forgave us. His sacrifice on the cross demonstrated his love and forgiveness in a way we could never repay. All we can do is receive it and thank him that he gives us the privilege of identifying with him in our own suffering, and forgive others as he has forgiven us.

QUESTIONS FOR REFLECTION AND DISCUSSION

- Which of the five points of suffering is the hardest for you to accept? Which one do you identify with the most?
- How have your past struggles and your suffering changed you? Did you become embittered, or did you become a better person?
- Landry Fields's god was the NBA. What gods have you had in your life? How did God deal with you in each situation?
- Explain how forgiveness is both a kind of suffering and also freeing.

9

What Happens If I'm Suffering and My Faith Isn't Enough?

Introduction

Throughout this book we have talked about a number of people who, in the prime of life, were confronted with a horrible and irreversible condition that eventually took their life or, short of that, set them on a lifelong journey of suffering. It's likely you know someone whose experience parallels the stories we've told. I (Stan) know such a person. He was my father.

At the age of twenty-four, my father was in his first year of graduate school at Wheaton College, preparing for a career as a pastor. That's when he and my mother received the devastating news that he had Hodgkin's disease (known as Hodgkin's lymphoma today). It was shocking to my young parents. Within two years my father would be gone, leaving my mother with four-year-old me.

For many years I was blissfully ignorant of the toll this ordeal took on our little family. My mother married again four years later, and the three of us had a pretty good life together, so I was never motivated to research my past. Only recently have I looked into what happened and how it affected my mother and father. Aided by the discovery of some letters from my suffering father to his parents, I have discovered the details of what he was experiencing. What I have learned is mildly disconcerting.

You see, my father never expected to die—at least not from his disease. He had been raised in a church that emphasized the power of healing, so immediately after his diagnosis—by then his cancer was quite advanced—my father was convinced that God would heal him, so much so that he refused medical treatment for a time.

"He seems to feel he should continue as he always has, by continuing in faith," his brother wrote to their parents. "The doctor thought he should begin treatment by tomorrow, but he does not want to undergo any surgery or X ray."

My father eventually received treatment, but it was too late. And since the first successful cures of his disease were not to come for another decade, we don't know if the results would have been any different had he followed the doctor's advice. It's not that my father didn't believe in doctors; he just believed in God more. He was so convinced that God was going to heal him that he lived with the expectation that his health would be restored, even as it dramatically declined. "We know He wants to deliver me," my father wrote.

The American Way

If you live in America, you're going to understand what we're about to discuss with you. If you live in another part of the world, particularly in a place where uncertainty and difficulties are a way of life, just relax and read. And feel free to be perplexed by what we silly Americans believe.

You can sum up American beliefs in what might be called the American Way. It's the can-do, whatever-it-takes spirit that pervades every part of American life. You see it in the boardrooms of companies, and you see it on soccer fields where the parents of eight-year-olds who don't yet care about winning act as if the world is going to end if their team isn't victorious. We Americans love rags-to-riches stories and possess a pull-yourself-up-from-your bootstraps attitude about life. There's no whining allowed—only winning. Second place is for losers. Michael Phelps is a national hero, but Tiger Woods is washed up, not because of his behavior, but because he committed the ultimate unpardonable sin—he stopped winning.

You might be wondering what all this has to do with sickness and suffering. To do that we need to give you a brief history lesson (stay with us, it will be worth it). America's optimistic attitude came from the Age of Enlightenment, which died in Europe with the French Revolution in 1789, but was reborn in America, thanks to Thomas Jefferson and the architects of the United States Constitution. These forefathers believed strongly in the rights and freedom of the individual. They were also predominantly deists, which meant they believed in a God who kept his distance from the affairs of men.

By the middle of the nineteenth century, a marriage between Enlightenment thinking and deism spawned the New Thought movement. Basically, the proponents of this philosophy believed all sickness originates in the mind and is a consequence of false beliefs. You can be what you want to be if you just think positively. It wasn't long before some church groups began incorporating elements of New Thought into their theology and practice. A turn-of-the-century pastor by the name of E. W. Kenyon put an "evangelical spin" on New Thought and taught Christians to believe that their minds and words could bring about either positive or negative results. Furthermore, God is more or less obligated to respond to your affirmations and requests, because after all, that's how faith works.

Death, the Prosperity Gospel, and Me

The result of this mishmash of positive thinking and faith has produced what is now commonly known as the prosperity gospel. "Put
simply," writes Kate Bowler, author of a widely circulated opinion
piece in the *New York Times* called "Death, the Prosperity Gospel
and Me," the prosperity gospel is "the belief that God grants health
and wealth to those with the right kind of faith." According to
Bowler, the prosperity gospel is characterized by phrases such as
"God is in me. God's ability is mine. God's strength is mine. God's
health is mine. His success is mine. I am a winner. I am a conqueror."[1]

The irony of Bowler's extensive research into the movement,
chronicled in her book *Blessed*, is that she is battling stage 4 cancer. At the age of thirty-five. (Now you get the title of her piece
in the *New York Times*.) To say the least, it's given her a unique
perspective on the way the American never-say-die optimism and
the prosperity gospel's mantra of "name it and claim it" combine
to convince people that God does not want you to suffer. Stan's
father certainly believed that. "We must be careful not to speak of
a disease I have, but of a disease I *had*," he wrote as he lay dying.

You may be wondering why we're picking on the prosperity
gospel in a book about suffering and evil. We have a response, and
it comes from (you guessed it) Kate Bowler: "The prosperity gospel
tries to solve the riddle of human suffering."[2] Bingo. That's why
we're interested in exploring this important topic. Not because
it's true, but because it claims to work. Because it claims in one
fell swoop to answer the questions we've been wrestling with in
this book.

And just how does it do that? "It offers people a guarantee,"
writes Bowler. "Follow these rules, and God will reward you, heal
you, restore you." It's a way of controlling God. Only it doesn't
work that way, does it? Bowler continues:

> The prosperity gospel holds to this illusion of control until the very
> end. If a believer gets sick and dies, shame compounds the grief.

Those who are loved and lost are just that—those who have lost the test of faith. In my work, I have heard countless stories of refusing to acknowledge that the end had finally come. An emaciated man was pushed about a mega church in a wheelchair as churchgoers declared that he was already healed. A woman danced around her sister's deathbed shouting to horrified family members that the body can yet live. There is no graceful death, no ars moriendi, in the prosperity gospel. There are only jarring disappointments after fevered attempts to deny its inevitability.[3]

QUESTIONS FOR REFLECTION AND DISCUSSION

- In what ways does the prosperity gospel attempt to solve "the riddle of human suffering"?
- How does the prosperity gospel try to control God?
- Did you look up the phrase *ars moriendi*? Reflect on what it means. Do Christians do this very well? Should they?

So How Does God Bless Us in Sickness and in Health?

Just because the word *blessed* is the "shorthand for the prosperity message," that doesn't mean it's a hollow promise. The concept of blessing is an important theme in Scripture. It's the cornerstone of Jesus' famous Sermon on the Mount. Notice those who Jesus says are blessed:

> "Blessed are the poor in spirit,
>   for theirs is the kingdom of heaven.
> Blessed are those who mourn,
>   for they will be comforted.
> Blessed are the meek,
>   for they will inherit the earth.
> Blessed are those who hunger and thirst for righteousness,
>   for they will be filled.
> Blessed are the merciful,
>   for they will be shown mercy.

137

> Blessed are the pure in heart,
> for they will see God.
> Blessed are the peacemakers,
> for they will be called children of God.
> Blessed are those who are persecuted because of
> righteousness,
> for theirs is the kingdom of heaven.

"Blessed are you when people insult you, persecute you and falsely say all kinds of evil against you because of me. Rejoice and be glad, because great is your reward in heaven, for in the same way they persecuted the prophets who were before you."

Matthew 5:3–12

Nothing about healing there. Or prosperity. Those who are blessed are those who are everything but healthy and wealthy. What Jesus has in mind is the ultimate well-being and spiritual joy (that's the *blessing* part) of those who have experienced God's salvation and who as a result are living in God's kingdom.

Does blessing ever include healing from sickness and suffering? We believe it does, but it's not healing on demand. We know God heals as he always has, so we pray for healing when sickness occurs, and we have faith that God can heal. But we also understand that God may, for reasons only he knows, choose not to restore our health.

All Will Be Well

Many years ago a friend of mine (Stan's) was diagnosed with a cancer that is almost always fatal. We were in a Bible study together, and when we learned of our friend's condition, we held a healing service in the spirit and direction of James 5:14–15:

> Is anyone among you sick? Let them call the elders of the church to pray over them and anoint them with oil in the name of the Lord. And the prayer offered in faith will make the sick person well; the Lord will raise them up. If they have sinned, they will be forgiven.

138

None of us had any doubts that God *could* heal our stricken friend. Still, there were those in our group who wondered if God *would* heal him. I was one of those.

Surgery was performed and the outlook was grim. We continued to pray, hoping for a miracle—but it was not to be. Our friend passed into eternity. There was deep sadness and some frustration that God had not done what we knew he *could* do. But there was also hope. Though God had not healed our friend physically, he had actually done much more.

I know this because my wife and I visited our friend one month before he died. When we walked into his home and saw him sitting in his favorite chair, we were startled, though we tried not to show it. His physical appearance had noticeably deteriorated. Yet there was a sparkle in his eye.

Not knowing what else to say, I asked my friend if he was disappointed that God had not healed him. I'll never forget his response. He looked right at me, struggled to sit up straight in his chair, and reprimanded me on the spot. "Oh, but God has healed me. He has healed me in ways you could not even imagine. I don't want you to worry about me. God is in control. All will be well." Then, without missing a beat, he gave a simple yet profoundly elegant explanation. "This is how God has healed me. He is using my life to touch others with his love. As long as I live, I want God to use me."

Indeed, God used our friend to shine his love on hundreds of people who visited him in the last weeks of his life, even as the insidious growth in his head continued to take its malicious toll. God had healed him, and through that healing, God showed all of us how much he cares for his frail and susceptible children.

What Kind of Faith Does It Take?

The story of Stan's friend vividly illustrates a principle expressed by J. I. Packer in his essay "Hoped-for Healing":

God uses chronic pain and weakness, along with other afflictions, as his chisel for sculpting our lives. Felt weakness deepens dependence on Christ for strength each day. The weaker we feel, the harder we lean. And the harder we lean, the stronger we grow spiritually, even while our bodies waste away.[4]

We've experienced this, and we suspect you have as well. And if you have, you understand the kind of faith it takes to endure and even benefit from suffering. It's a faith that believes even though it's dark, a faith that understands that just because God doesn't heal us physically or make our lives more comfortable doesn't mean he is not at work. The fact that God is an active agent in the world—the belief of *theism* as opposed to *deism*—means that he is able to work all things, even the things we consider bad, for our good. Realizing that should change the way we pursue health and face calamities in our lives. Rather than hoping for only one good outcome—the restoration of our health or finances or whatever—we need to be open to other outcomes, even if they aren't what we hope and pray for. If God is truly good, shouldn't we trust him and accept the possibility that he may be using our suffering for another kind of "good"?

QUESTIONS FOR REFLECTION AND DISCUSSION

• How do you normally use the word *blessed*? Do you ever use it when things aren't going well? Why or why not?

• Look up the Bible's definition of faith in Hebrews 11:1. Is this consistent with having a faith that believes in the dark? How so?

• Was there ever a time when the "good" God gave you was different from the "good" you asked for? In what ways was God's good better than yours?

A Time to Weep

Dave Furman understands this all too well. For more than ten years he has lived with a debilitating condition whereby the nerves in his arms don't work properly. He is in constant pain, and nothing the doctors have done—procedures, surgeries, therapy, drugs—has worked. Furman, who is a pastor, needs help to do things we take for granted, such as buttoning his shirt or buckling a seat belt.

In his moving book, *Being There*, Furman is candid about the depression he experienced and the resentment he harbored as he tried to cope with his agonizing condition. It would be easy for him to wallow in self-pity, or worse, try to suppress his fears and grief "instead of dealing with it in healthy and honest ways."[5] But Furman has chosen a different way, one that involves sorrow and lament. "Often in the church Christians are taught that weeping is failing to trust God," he writes. "There is seldom a place for sorrow and lamentation among Christians—no freedom to cry out to the Lord. However, the book of Psalms is filled with what are called psalms of lament."[6]

Furman encourages us to "weep honestly at the loss we've experienced." Of course, he prays for relief from his pain, but he takes comfort in the fact that honest weeping "is fundamentally grounded in hope."[7]

Hello, darkness, my old friend

Both Furman and Tim Keller reference Psalm 88, the darkest of all the psalms of lament. Other psalms in this category end on an upbeat note, but not this one. The last line is stark and maybe even a bit sarcastic in its tone: "darkness is my closest friend." Furman and Keller identify some lessons we can draw from Psalm 88:

- *It's possible to stay in darkness for a long time.* This has been the case with Furman, and he knows he's not the only one. "I've talked to many families that have been affected by chronic pain, disability, sickness, loss, and depression."[8]
- *It's okay to express anger in the midst of our despair.* Keller points out that Job "tore his robe" and "fell to the ground" (Job 1:20) when he heard he had lost everything.[9] Yet in his

dark anguish he didn't sin (see verse 22). If you are hurting, don't listen to anyone telling you to trust God more or criticizing you for not having enough faith. God is okay with your lamentable behavior.

- *In darkness we learn to love God for himself and not for his benefits.* When we come to the end of ourselves because of our suffering, something wonderful happens. We begin to appreciate God for who he is, not for what he can do for us. At the end of his ordeal, Job said, "My ears had heard of you but now I have seen you" (Job 42:5). Like so many of us, Job had heard about God, but now he saw him through his experience and the eyes of faith and spiritual understanding. He saw God for who he really is, not for who he wanted him to be. He accepted what God permits and what he ordains, including suffering.

With most people—and this has been our experience—the darkness eventually gives way to light. When that happens, our sorrow is turned into strength, and our desire for external happiness is replaced by a deep contentment in God himself. We are, as Ernest Hemingway famously said, "strong in the broken places."[10]

The Darkness of Jesus

If there's a constant theme that emerges in this discussion about faith and suffering, it's this: *We don't have enough faith to see us through the hard times.* The prosperity gospel (for the most part) treats faith as a commodity, and a lot of us have been caught up in this at times. We engage faith when we need it and wait for God to fix things.

As we have discussed, that's an approach that often ends in disappointment, because it is based on being in control. That's not what we sign up for when we believe in God by faith and continue to live by faith in his grace. The Christian life is about *surrender,* not control. Faith is not about manipulating circumstances so they stack in our favor. It's about trusting God no matter what. It's his will, not ours.

The kind of faith we need to have when darkness has invaded our lives is to put everything at the feet of Jesus. He is the only object our faith needs, not just because he died for our sins, but because of what he experienced before it was finished. Keller talks about "the darkness of Jesus" in that Jesus truly experienced ultimate darkness. Keller refers to the last verse of Psalm 39, another psalm of lament, where David writes, "Look away from me."

This dark lament eerily foreshadows the rejection Jesus would feel in the last moments on the cross, when God looked away. "He really was abandoned by God," Keller writes. "At the moment he died everyone had betrayed, denied, rejected, or forsaken him, even his Father. Total darkness was indeed Jesus' only friend."[11]

Jesus' experience of abandonment means that he will never abandon us. He took on the rejection we deserve. This is where faith leads us, to realize that even in the darkness, we can trust the Lord, who says, "Never will I leave you, never will I forsake you" (Hebrews 13:5).

QUESTIONS FOR REFLECTION AND DISCUSSION

- What does it mean for a Christian to lament? Why are we reluctant to cry out to the Lord?
- Read Psalm 88 in its entirety. What are your impressions? What do you think of the ending?
- How does the darkness of Jesus help you? How does Jesus model faith for you?

What *Not* to Tell Someone Who's Hurting

If you are currently going through a dark period, or if you've experienced a calamity in the past, you have probably heard comments from (well-intentioned) people that were not helpful. Some may have even been hurtful. We've encountered a few ourselves, as have some of the writers we've read while writing this book. In order to help us all do better when it comes to encouraging rather than discouraging those who are hurting, here is our unofficial top ten list of what *not* to say.

1. *Don't tell them to remember Romans 8:28.* Okay, this is a pivotal verse when it comes to understanding God's perspective on our problems, and we have quoted it more than once in this book. Because God is both sovereign and loving, he really does cause all things to work together for our good if we love him. But this is something for each of us to believe and trust, not to wave like some spiritual wand over someone who is in the throes of badness—especially if things are going well for you when you quote the verse.

2. *Don't tell them that what they are experiencing is keeping them from going through something worse.* There's some truth to this. Isaiah 57:1 says, "The righteous are taken away to be spared from evil." But saying or even thinking that someone is suffering now so they won't face something worse down the line (like death, for example?) is beyond inappropriate. Only God knows what lies ahead.

3. *Don't tell them their affliction must be a punishment for some sin.* Only a clueless (and, we would add, *hypocritical*) jerk would say this to someone personally. But how often have you heard a prominent Christian say something like this when tragedy strikes on a larger scale—such as a natural disaster or a mass shooting? We should all cringe and ask for forgiveness on behalf of these people. Of course, this isn't a recent phenomenon. Jesus heard the same response to a tragedy from his disciples, who asked him if the victims of a freak accident died because of their sin. Jesus replied emphatically, "I tell you, no! But unless you repent, you will all perish" (Luke 13:5). *Touché*, Jesus.

4. *Don't tell them how special they are for going through difficult times.* This one is tricky, because it's meant to be a compliment. The idea comes from Paul: "No test or temptation that comes your way is beyond the course of what others have had to face. All you need to remember is that God will never let you down; he'll never let you be pushed past your limit; he'll always be there to help you come through it" (1 Corinthians 10:13 THE MESSAGE). By implication, we think someone who is going through a really tough time must have a higher pain threshold than we do, or else God wouldn't allow it. Our advice is to let people figure that out for themselves. They don't need to hear it from you.

5. *Don't tell them you know how they feel.* It's amazing how some guy can make your suffering all about him. "I'm so sorry you have stage 4 cancer. I had a friend who had stage 5 cancer. Wow, that was rough." Don't be that guy.

6. *Don't be super spiritual.* This includes quoting Bible verses like Romans 8:28, saying stuff like "Don't worry, God is in control," or repeating the worst line ever, "You're sad now, but just think—she's in a better place!" We don't even know how to respond to that.

7. *Don't ask too many questions.* We humans are naturally inquisitive, but asking a lot of questions of someone who has just lost a loved one is just wrong. Instead of probing for details, provide support. Rather than feeding your curiosity, show love, even if you don't say anything at all.

8. *Don't pay lip service.* We're all guilty of this one. This is where we say something like "Let me know if you need anything," or "Don't hesitate to call me." These kinds of empty gestures are pretty worthless. "If you really want to help a hurting friend," advises Dave Furman, "then offer to help in a specific way."[12]

9. *Don't tell them to "move on" with their lives.* This goes back to the American Way (or maybe the British Way) of putting

the past behind and pushing forward. You know, stiff upper lip and all that. Telling someone to get over their grief is not only insensitive, but potentially harmful. We all process suffering and loss in our own way. The teacher in Ecclesiastes wisely says, "There is a time to weep."

10. *Don't avoid them.* We get this one. Being around people who are hurting makes us uncomfortable. We may say we just want to give grieving people their space, but really we're just avoiding them. Sympathy cards are appropriate, but don't let that be all you say or do. Follow up at the appropriate time. Send an email or text just to say you're thinking about and praying for them. Then do just that.

Become a Hope-Dealer

We've given you ten approaches to those who are hurting that won't work. How about one approach that will? After eight years of living with pain in his arms, Dave Furman says there was just one thing that helped him through his dark nights. "The short answer is that God delivered me from the darkness of despair through my friends and family as they shared their hope with me." Furman refers to this group of people as "hope-dealers."[13]

If you're going through some dark times right now, and you don't believe your faith is enough to get you through, don't despair. Allow or even invite others to bring you hope. And if you know someone who is hurting, take it upon yourself to give them hope. You'll be what Furman calls a "hope-dealer." It doesn't take any training. Just show love in small but personal ways, and when necessary, use words. Most of all, be a silent presence. It's relatively easy to send cards and emails, but when you visit someone and just sit with them with no agenda except to be there, you've become a one hundred percent certified hope-dealer.

For Furman, the cadre of hope-dealers who surrounded him reminded him of "what Christ endured in order to bring me to

God. . . . In those dark nights of the soul, the joyful truth they shared with me rang in my ears."[14]

QUESTIONS FOR REFLECTION AND DISCUSSION

- How many of the ten approaches to hurting people have you used? How many have you heard when you were hurting?
- What is the best thing anyone ever did for you when you were hurting?

10

What Can I Do About Suffering and Evil?

Introduction

There wasn't a more popular teacher at Christ Presbyterian Academy in Nashville than Ben Ellis. So when he was diagnosed with esophageal cancer, Ben's family, friends, co-workers, and students struggled with the bleak prognosis. People with this type of cancer typically don't live more than eighteen months. In fact, Ben died less than a year from the time of his diagnosis.

Like many of us would do, Ben asked God to extend his life, but he didn't do it for himself. He wanted more time so that he could reach as many people as possible to show the love of Jesus through his suffering. God answered his request in a way no one could have imagined.

Just a few weeks before Ben died, four hundred high school students, teachers, and administrators from Christ Presbyterian Academy showed up at his house and proceeded to sing worship songs from his front lawn. Ben opened his window and sang along. Someone captured this beautiful moment on video and shared it with friends, one of whom sent it to country singer Tim McGraw, who posted it on his Facebook page. Within days the video went viral. As quoted in a blog post by Russ Ramsey, a pastor at Christ Presbyterian Church, here's what Ben wrote in his CaringBridge journal after that impromptu time of worship at his house:

> Remember my prayer request [for more days] from my post on August 20? God has blown the doors off this prayer request! This is far beyond our wildest, biggest dreams. I have never felt so weak, but God is strong in me. More days, more glory to him, more people seeing Jesus, more people coming to know Jesus. What an amazing answer to prayer![1]

Ben died ten days after the Facebook posting. By then, the video had been viewed more than thirty-two million times. Millions of additional views occurred after his death. At the apex of his pain and struggle, Ben had demonstrated to millions of people that the presence and love of Christ transcend gruesome suffering.

We Want to Respond, but How?

The preceding nine chapters of this book have dealt primarily with the philosophical and theological aspects of suffering and evil. We don't expect that all of your questions have been answered, but hopefully your cerebral cortex has been stimulated. (You're welcome.) As this book concludes, we move to a more personal and practical perspective: What can any of us do to alleviate the suffering that exists in the world?

Evidence of pain, suffering, and evil haunts all of us on a daily basis. As this chapter is being written:

- After the devastation of Hurricane Matthew in Haiti in 2016, the death toll was 478 and an estimated 350,000 people were left in need of assistance.[2]
- After two and a half years in captivity, dozens of young women have been released by Boko Haram, the radical Islamist group

150

that kidnapped 276 Nigerian school girls from their dormitory in the dead of night in April 2014. Previously, a few girls had escaped, and some have been reported as killed, but the majority of the girls are still missing.[3]

- The World Food Programme estimated that 4.8 million people in South Sudan—representing about 40 percent of the country's population—are going hungry due to drought conditions that will likely intensify.[4]

The frequency of atrocities—those caused by nature and those caused by humanity—seems to be increasing. Our sympathies are evoked as we read these reports and hear the anecdotal stories of the families devastated by these events across the globe. But realistically, what can any single individual do to relieve such suffering and injustices?

QUESTIONS FOR REFLECTION AND DISCUSSION

- What catastrophes and tragedies from around the world weigh heavy on your heart?
- Have you found a way to participate in the relief of that suffering or in the opposition of that evil?
- Within your own community of family and friends and church, are you connected with people who live with constant pain and hardship? How do they deal with it? Are you able to provide any assistance?

As Christians think about trying to make even the tiniest positive impact on global suffering—far or near—we often feel overwhelmed by our incapacity to make a constructive contribution. We end up doing very little, or nothing at all. But maybe our aspirations are too big. Instead of merely thinking about doing something great for God around the world, perhaps we should change our approach and actually engage in doing something small for God in the course of our everyday lives. We can respond to suffering and evil in the world by starting at the local level.

Perhaps your greatest impact can be made by modeling in your own life, and proclaiming from your own experience, the joy and hope that are found in Christ despite the challenge of pain and suffering. Eliminating the causes of suffering is a lofty and noble goal that should not be abandoned. But the more likely scenario for Christians is that we will have personal encounters that allow us to present Christ as the Comforter of those who are suffering. Before that can be done effectively (and confidently), however, you must have a firm grasp of God's perspective on suffering. We've talked a lot about this in the preceding nine chapters, so consider this a review, and perhaps another step in the process of trying your best to understand what God is up to in this broken world.

> ### QUESTIONS FOR REFLECTION AND DISCUSSION
>
> In the next few paragraphs, we'll be reviewing, and amplifying, biblical principles about suffering and evil that we covered in the rest of the book.
>
> • What principles do you remember?
> • Are there some that you are still uncertain about?
>
> This is not an open-book quiz, but we won't know if you cheat by glancing at some of the earlier chapters.

A Biblical Theology of Suffering

You likely wouldn't be reading this book if it was emblazoned with "A Biblical Theology of Suffering" across the front cover. Granted, that title is not particularly engaging, but it would have been accurate. *Theology* simply refers to "the study of God and of God's relation to the world."[5] Attempting to understand God's perspective on the specific issue of human pain and hardship would be the *theology of suffering*. We add the adjective *biblical* to identify the definitive source of information on the topic.

Having a biblical theology of suffering is essential for many reasons, not the least of which are these:

- When you are having your own problems, Satan will mess with your head. He'll make you think that your current struggles are your fault, that God is punishing you, that relief will never come to a miserable wretch like yourself; and he'll have you fixated on the "why me" question. But a biblical theology of suffering will allow you to dismiss such errant thinking in order to turn your thoughts off of yourself and onto Christ.

> "So do not fear, for I am with you; do not be dismayed, for I am your God. I will strengthen you and help you; I will uphold you with my righteous right hand."
>
> Isaiah 41:10

- Every Christian should be fluent on this topic because we are all surrounded by people who are enduring pain of some type. When people are hurting, they need to be comforted, and you can be the one who ministers to them in this way because you have experienced it yourself.

> Praise be to the God and Father of our Lord Jesus Christ, the Father of compassion and the God of all comfort, who comforts us in all our troubles, *so that we can comfort those in any trouble with the comfort we ourselves receive from God.*
>
> 2 Corinthians 1:3–4, emphasis added

Volumes could be written on the biblical theology of suffering. What follows is an overview of four principles that you can apply personally in your own times of adversity and that you can use to comfort others when they are suffering.

153

Suffering Is Not a Question of *If* but of *When*

Contrary to those who preach a happy-clappy, carefree kind of Christianity, Jesus promised just the opposite for his followers: "In this world you will have trouble. But take heart! I have overcome the world" (John 16:33). Notice the absence of any equivocation in that statement. "You *will* have trouble." It is guaranteed. You can count on it. And if you haven't suffered yet, then get ready, because it is coming.

The certainty of suffering for Christians is mentioned by James in his letter. The topic sentence that immediately follows the greeting is "Consider it pure joy, my brothers and sisters, whenever you face trials of many kinds . . ." (James 1:2). This is the classic *when*, not *if*, promise of suffering.

James wrote his epistle primarily to Jewish Christians who had fled Jerusalem due to severe persecution and resettled in Gentile communities throughout Asia Minor. So when James wrote, "You will face trials," no one would have disputed the certitude of his statement. But because this promise of travails applies to all Christians, including those in the twenty-first century, James mentions that the adversity will differ on a case-by-case basis; everyone will suffer, but there will be "many kinds" of trials.

Here is the bottom line: Although the form, duration, frequency, and severity may differ, every Christian will experience suffering. There are no exceptions to the rule. Suffering is the rule.

Suffering Is a Good Thing

Why does God make suffering a seemingly mandatory component of the Christian life? Apparently because suffering is essential for our spiritual growth process. As theologian D. A. Carson puts it, "There is a certain kind of maturity that can be attained only through the discipline of suffering."[6] Citing Hebrews 4 and 5, Carson explains that even Jesus learned from what he suffered, which

154

equipped him to be for us a high priest who is able "to empathize with our weaknesses" (Hebrews 4:15).

Pastor and author John Stumbo found these verses from Hebrews to be a helpful reminder that suffering is a useful tool used by God in the lives of his children. Stumbo knows about suffering because he had a mysterious illness for almost two years, during which time he lost muscle strength and the ability to swallow. Imagine no food or liquids by mouth; he couldn't even swallow his own saliva. He says that there was a drastic change in his perspective when he began to view his suffering as a tool for becoming more like Jesus. Here are the steps in the process he experienced:

1. *In the midst of his suffering, he began to have greater hope.* "Knowing that God will not waste this pain but use it for good in my life, lifts my head and my heart to better places."[7]

2. *With greater hope, he began to anticipate and expect changes in his spiritual life that Christ was accomplishing through his physical pain.* "Since the trials are a refining fire, I look through the flames to see glimpses of a new character emerging."[8]

3. *Hope and expectancy can produce joy while the pain persists.* "Believing with all our being that great good arises out of great hardship, and desiring nothing on earth more than seeing the life of Christ lived through us, we can experience an otherworldly joy in adversity."[9]

The epistle of James mentions a similar building-block benefit from suffering. You'll remember James 1:2 from a few pages ago, which is the preface to James's explanation:

Consider it pure joy, my brothers and sisters, whenever you face trials of many kinds, because you know that the testing of your faith produces perseverance. Let perseverance finish its work so that you may be mature and complete, not lacking anything.

James 1:2–4

James presents an oxymoron: joyful suffering. He isn't saying that we should face our pain *with* joy; rather, we should consider our suffering *to be* joy. In other words, we should find the process of our suffering to be a joyful experience. It is easily said, but is it realistic to be joyful if your suffering is of the cancer variety, or a broken marriage, or the death of a child?

James gives the answer for finding joy in suffering when he refers to "the testing of your faith" and "perseverance." Like John Stumbo referring to suffering as a tool God uses, James sees suffering as a way of building up our faith. The stronger our faith becomes, the more we can persevere. As we experience increased perseverance in suffering, we realize the authenticity of our faith. Knowing and experiencing genuineness of faith in God produces joy—joy that arises because of, and in the midst of, suffering.

It's All About Christ's Purpose in the Pain, Not the Cause of the Pain

When Jesus walked the earth, he encountered a lot of people who were suffering. Take your pick: blind, lame, crippled, paralyzed, demon possessed, dead. The list goes on. Jesus never talked with these people about what caused their disability. But the disciples raised the question once. In keeping with the philosophy of their culture, they assumed that rich people were rich because they had God's favor; conversely, it was the common notion that physical defects and deformities were the result of God's punishment for sins committed by the person himself, or by the person's parents. Jesus took the opportunity to correct their erroneous theology of suffering:

> As he went along, he saw a man blind from birth. His disciples asked him, "Rabbi, who sinned, this man or his parents, that he was born blind?"
>
> "Neither this man nor his parents sinned," said Jesus, "but this happened so that the works of God might be displayed in him."
>
> John 9:1–3

Two principles in the biblical theology of suffering are present in this brief interchange:

- While we sometimes cause our own hardship, much of the time the bad stuff that happens isn't our fault (like natural disasters, disease, birth deformities, which are just the effects of a world broken by sin in general). Jesus corrected the disciples' misunderstanding about all of this by declaring that the blind man's suffering was not the direct result of a specific sin; bad circumstances are seldom a sign of God's punishment.

- God is a master at taking a bad situation and using it to display his glory. The passage in John goes on to describe how Jesus restored sight to this beggar. In the process, the beggar's spiritual vision was healed, as he gave this report to the antagonistic Jewish leaders: "Nobody has ever heard of opening the eyes of a man born blind. If this man were not from God, he could do nothing" (John 9:32–33). That's the lesson that Jesus wanted the disciples to remember— not what caused the suffering, but who conquered the suffering.

Paul addresses the same principle: God can create a beautiful result out of any and every ugly situation. Here is how Paul explains it: "And we know that God causes everything to work together for the good of those who love God and are called according to his purpose for them" (Romans 8:28 NLT). This verse explains that God can and does work in tragic circumstances *for the good* of those who love him. But the "good" that God accomplishes may not necessarily involve fixing what is broken. This promise does *not* say that God makes everything good. He won't automatically get you a new job after you have been laid off; this is not a guarantee that every failed marriage will be restored; Alzheimer's disease may continue its downward spiral.

From God's perspective, the best outcome for you is when the difficult circumstances cause you to be more dependent upon God, seeking him more, and growing stronger in your relationship with him. The "good" that God promises to bring out of your tough situation in Romans 8:28 is described in verse 29 as your being "conformed to the image of his Son." In other words, God can use the suffering we endure as a process that results in our becoming more Christlike.

He wants us to look beyond our present circumstances to the goal of a deeper relationship with him. When we have that perspective, the *cause* or the *why* of our suffering will be inconsequential. As Paul states in this same passage: "Yet what we suffer now is nothing compared to the glory he will reveal to us later" (Romans 8:18 NLT).

Our Concern for the Suffering of Others Should Be a Top Priority

If we truly love Jesus, we will want to be like him. We should want our hearts to be sensitive to the things that he cares about. Our time, treasure, and talents should be devoted to those things that Jesus considers to have eternal significance.

Read Matthew 25:31–46 for proof of what matters to God. Be prepared for a dose of spiritual reality when you read this passage, because it draws a sharp contrast between two groups of people: those who are invited into the eternal kingdom, and those who are relegated to eternal punishment. The difference was in the authenticity of the faith of each group. It was easy for Jesus to determine if their faith was genuine—he looked to see if their priorities during life were aligned with his. To the heaven-bound group, Jesus said,

> "Come, you who are blessed by my Father; take your inheritance, the kingdom prepared for you since the creation of the world. For I was hungry and you gave me something to eat, I was thirsty and you gave me something to drink, I was a stranger and you invited

me in, I needed clothes and you clothed me, I was sick and you looked after me, I was in prison and you came to visit me."

Matthew 25:34–36

Jesus was speaking figuratively; the people Jesus was addressing hadn't shown kindness to him, but when they did it to "the least of these," it was as if they were serving him. In other words, the simple, loving acts of kindness extended to the forgotten members of society are reflective of a heart that is aligned with God's priorities.

For the hell-bound group, the opposite was true. They heard these harsh words:

"Depart from me, you who are cursed, into the eternal fire prepared for the devil and his angels. For I was hungry and you gave me nothing to eat, I was thirsty and you gave me nothing to drink, I was a stranger and you did not invite me in, I needed clothes and you did not clothe me, I was sick and in prison and you did not look after me."

Matthew 25:41–43

As a result of this group's callous attitude toward the disadvantaged—an attitude that revealed an absence of the love of God in their hearts—they went away to eternal punishment.

The biblical theology of suffering contemplates a compassionate Christianity that seeks to care for the impoverished, the impaired, and the deprived. These are the people who are often forgotten and left alone by the more prosperous members of society. They may be considered as unlovely, but they are loved by God. As Christians, we are called to relieve their suffering. It is not complicated. It doesn't have to be expensive. It can be as easy as . . .

- giving a drink of water to someone who is thirsty;
- feeding the hungry;
- giving nice clothes to someone whose only apparel is frayed and tattered; or
- showing hospitality to the homeless and the forgotten elderly.

159

- Make a list of the church ministries and community programs known to you that are relieving the suffering in your city.
- Next, make a list of similar groups that seek to alleviate suffering around the world.
- Where does God want you to be involved?

When Your Theology of Suffering Becomes Contagious

Let's finish this chapter where it started, by asking the question of what can be done, on a personal level and in a tangible way, to relieve the suffering that exists in the world. For purposes of this discussion, we'll rule out inventing a cure for cancer or eradicating the Colombian drug cartel. For most of us Christians, God isn't calling us to change the world for all people. But he is asking us to change the world for a few people.

We suggested earlier that the greatest impact on a personal level might be achieved not by seeking to eliminate all of the world's suffering and evil, but by allowing people to experience joy in the midst of their suffering and pain. That won't happen by wishful thinking. But "show and tell" works, and it's biblical, too:

> Always be prepared to give an answer to everyone who asks you to give the reason for the hope that you have. But do this with gentleness and respect.
>
> 1 Peter 3:15

This verse is deceptively simple in its explanation of lifestyle evangelism.

- Peter is encouraging Christians to put their lives on display for the world to see. This will require relationships with other people that are deep enough so that they see how you respond to the hardships in your life. Let your biblical perspective

160

of theology be apparent to others. Surprise them with the oxymoronic miracle of finding joy in your suffering.

- Because your experience will contrast with the way they handle suffering, they might ask you for an explanation.
- You won't ignore or dodge the question. You will "be prepared to give an answer" why you have hope while tribulation swirls around you. You have knowledge and personal experience of how God uses suffering in your life to reveal his presence.
- You won't need to be defensive. You know you have an answer that will relieve them of anxiety. You will simply respond to their questions with an attitude of "gentleness and respect."

It is our prayer for you that your life might reflect a biblical theology of suffering that is contagious. May the story of your life—particularly the manner in which you deal with various troubles that you experience—be so engaging that other people want to catch what you've got.

What Jesus Wants for You

David Ireland had a personal theology of suffering that was contagious. His circumstances were bleak, but the way he responded to them was appealing. David and his wife, Joyce, were a young married couple, excited about Joyce's pregnancy, despite the fact that David had previously been diagnosed with a crippling neurological disease. Facing an imminent death with the prospects of not living long enough to see his own child born, David wrote a series of thirteen letters to the child who was residing in Joyce's womb. These letters, subsequently published as *Letters to an Unborn Child*, are a father's gift of life lessons about growing up, romance, marriage, and faith. Interspersed in the letters are references to the progressive, debilitating (and eventually fatal) effects of David's disease. David's personal, contagious theology of suffering leaps off the pages that he wrote to his unborn child:

> Today when I'm asked, "Do you believe God will heal you?" my response is a question, one I have asked myself. "Do I really need to be healed?" It's a genuine question, not a mere defense to avoid the issue. I'm firmly convinced that God is extremely good and that He does love and understand all the world and all the people in it. Does He want to heal me? I can't even answer that. My faith is in the genuineness of God, not in whether He will do this or that to demonstrate his goodness. I don't need acts of benevolence or wondrous words to prove it to me. That's not the nature of my relationship to God.
>
> Somehow—maybe because I have tasted the goodness and love of God in the experience of my conversion—I know that *God does not wish me evil*. I always end up there. It does not exclude the doubts but transcends them—ultimately overshadows them—the reality of what the God of creation must be like.
>
> Today your father's religious beliefs remain within the Christian tradition. I have deep personal connections with respect to the life, death, and resurrection of Jesus Christ. . . . What has enabled me to retain a Christian theology is the fact that over a period of years I have come to understand better, I think, the kind of person Jesus of Nazareth was. It is out of this understanding that I deeply affirm to you: God is believable and good.[10]

Your own circumstances may not result in a Facebook video that has millions of downloads. A book may never be written about the hardships you have endured. But the extent to which your suffering gets publicized should not be your concern. Jesus wants you to care for the poor, give food to the hungry, give water to those who are thirsty. Relieve them from their suffering. Then, when suffering falls upon you, which it will, use it as another opportunity to see Christ at work in your life. And may others be drawn to Christ in the process.

QUESTIONS FOR REFLECTION AND DISCUSSION

- Do you think Christians have a reputation for exhibiting gentleness and respect? Why or why not?

- Can you envision yourself responding to a genuine question about how your faith affects your daily life?

- If yes, describe how you might respond. If no, then identify the obstacles that would prevent you from doing so.

Notes

Chapter 1: If God Created Everything, Did He Create Evil?

1. Timothy Keller, *Walking with God through Pain and Suffering* (New York: Riverhead, 2013), 85–86.

2. Ibid.

3. Nicky Gumbel, "Experience Alpha" (lecture, Holy Trinity Brompton, London, September 28, 2015).

4. Istvan Bodnar, "Aristotle's Natural Philosophy," *Stanford Encyclopedia of Philosophy* (Winter 2016), ed. Edward N. Zalta, http://plato.stanford.edu/entries/aristotle-natphil/.

5. Frank Turek, *Stealing from God: Why Atheists Need God to Make Their Case* (Colorado Springs: NavPress, 2014), 117.

6. Randy Alcorn, *The Goodness of God: Assurance of Purpose in the Midst of Suffering* (Colorado Springs: Multnomah, 2010), 10.

7. Matt Chandler, "Our Story in Exodus," *Exodus* sermon series, The Village Church, August 21, 2016, http://www.thevillagechurch.net/resources/sermons/detail/our-story-in-exodus/.

8. Alvin Plantinga, *God, Freedom, and Evil* (Grand Rapids, MI: Eerdmans, 1977), 29.

9. C. S. Lewis, *The Problem of Pain* (New York: Macmillan, 1962), 69.

10. Alvin Plantinga, *God, Freedom, and Evil*, 29.

Chapter 2: Why Is There Suffering and Evil in a World Made Good by God?

1. C. S. Lewis, *A Grief Observed* (San Francisco, CA: HarperSanFrancisco, 1961), 6.

2. Ibid.

3. Annie Dillard, *For the Time Being* (New York: Vintage Books, 2000), 3.

4. Lewis, *A Grief Observed*, 6–7.

5. Ibid., 29.

6. Philip Yancey, *Disappointment with God* (Grand Rapids, MI: Zondervan, 1988), 48–49.

7. Ibid., 49.

8. Ibid., 50–51.

9. Ibid., 51.

10. Bruce Bickel and Stan Jantz, *Answering the Toughest Questions About God and the Bible* (Minneapolis: Bethany House, 2016), 57.

11. Yancey, *Disappointment with God*, 52.

12. Lewis, *A Grief Observed*, 22–33.

13. Ibid., 38.

14. Keller, *Walking with God*, 115.

15. Os Guinness, "When We Don't Know Why, We Trust God Who Knows Why," in *Be Still My Soul*, ed. Nancy Guthrie (Wheaton, IL: Crossway, 2010), 38.

16. Ibid., 38–39.

17. Kara Tippetts, *The Hardest Peace: Expecting Grace in the Midst of Life's Hard* (Colorado Springs: David C. Cook, 2014), 115.

Chapter 3: Why Doesn't God Eliminate Suffering and Evil?

1. Bruce Bickel and Stan Jantz, *Evidence for Faith 101* (Eugene, OR: Harvest House, 2008), 181–184.

2. Sean McDowell and Jonathan Morrow, *Is God Just a Human Invention? And Seventeen Other Questions Raised by the New Atheists* (Grand Rapids, MI: Kregel, 2010), 214.

3. Peter Kreeft, quoted in Lee Strobel, *The Case for Faith: A Journalist Investigates the Toughest Objections to Christianity* (Grand Rapids, MI: Zondervan, 2000), 51.

4. Keller, *Walking with God*, 101.

5. Wilson Benton Jr., "A Profound Answer to the Pressing Question, 'Why?'" in Guthrie, *Be Still My Soul*, 59.

6. Ibid.

7. Ibid., 59–60.

8. Ravi Zacharias and Vince Vitale, *Why Suffering? Finding Meaning and Comfort When Life Doesn't Make Sense* (New York: FaithWords, 2014), 117.

9. Ibid., 130.

10. Keller, *Walking with God*, 103.

11. Ibid., 107.

12. McDowell and Morrow, *Just a Human Invention?*, 216.

13. Lewis, *The Problem of Pain*, 93.

14. "Joni Eareckson Tada on Something Greater than Healing," interview by Sarah Pulliam Bailey, *Christianity Today*, October 8, 2010, http://www.christianity today.com/ct/2010/october/12.30.html.

Chapter 4: Why Is the Bible So Full of Violence?

1. *Wikipedia*, s.v. "Buddhism and Violence," last modified April 7, 2017, https://en.wikipedia.org/wiki/Buddhism_and_violence.

2. *Wikipedia*, s.v. "Violence Against Muslims in India" last modified April 7, 2017, https://en.wikipedia.org/wiki/Violence_against_Muslims_in_India.

3. Richard Dawkins, *The God Delusion* (New York: Houghton Mifflin, 2008), 280.

4. Ibid., 51.

5. Richard L. Strauss, *The Joy of Knowing God* (Neptune, NJ: Loizeaux Brothers, 1984), 140.

6. A. W. Tozer, "God's True and Just Judgments," Tozer Devotional online, accessed October 30, 2016, https://www.cmalliance.org/devotions/tozer?id=1193.

7. A. W. Pink, *The Attributes of God* (Swengel, PA: Reiner, 1968), 75.

8. Ibid., 76.

9. D. A. Carson, "God's Love and God's Wrath," *Bibliotheca Sacra* 156 (October–December 1999), 390 (emphasis added).

10. Ibid.

Chapter 5: Does God Care That the World Is Falling Apart?

1. Amy Hall, "Christians, You Will Suffer," *Stand to Reason* (blog), March 25, 2015, http://str.typepad.com/weblog/2015/03/christians-you-will-suffer.html.

2. Ibid.

3. *Oxford English Dictionary*, s.v. "deism," accessed April 18, 2017, https://en.oxforddictionaries.com/definition/us/deism.

4. *Dictionary.com Unabridged*, s.v. "deism," accessed April 18, 2017, http://www.dictionary.com/browse/deism.

5. Gemma Hunt, "Who Is Jesus?", *Alpha Film Series: Begin the Greatest Adventure*, episode 2, directed by Daniel H. A. Stewart (London: AFS Pictures LTD, 2016), DVD.

6. Alcorn, *Goodness of God*, 2.

Chapter 6: Why Do the Innocent Suffer?

1. Makoto Fujimura, *Silence and Beauty: Hidden Faith Born of Suffering* (Downers Grove, IL: InterVarsity Press, 2016), 46.

2. Peter Kreeft, *Making Sense Out of Suffering* (Cincinnati: Servant Books, 1986), 115.

3. Ibid., 107.

4. Ibid., 115.

5. Ibid., 116.

6. Fujimura, *Silence and Beauty*, 46.

7. John S. Feinberg, *When There Are No Easy Answers: Thinking Differently About God, Suffering and Evil, and Evil* (Grand Rapids, MI: Kregel, 2016), 37.

8. Ibid., 76.

9. Ibid., 77.

10. Ibid., 78.

11. Ibid., 94.

12. Ibid.

13. Ibid., 95–96.

Chapter 7: Is There a Difference between the Evil in the World
and the Sin in Me?

1. Douglas Linder, "The Nuremberg Trials," Famous Trials series, Jurist, December 2000, http://www.jurist.org/j20/famoustrials/nuremberg-trials.php.
2. Ibid.
3. Cornelius Plantinga Jr., *Not the Way It's Supposed to Be: A Breviary of Sin* (Grand Rapids, MI: Eerdmans, 1995), 21.
4. Ibid., 10.
5. Marguerite Shuster, *The Fall and Sin: What We Have Become as Sinners* (Grand Rapids, MI: Eerdmans, 2004),104.
6. Ibid., 101.
7. Ibid., 263–65.
8. Ibid., 125.
9. Cornelius Plantinga, *Not the Way It's Supposed to Be*, 40.
10. Ibid., 44–45.
11. Moses Hayyim Luzzatto [Moshe Chaim Luzzatto], trans. Mordecai Menahem Kaplan, *Mesillat Yesharim: The Path of the Upright* (Philadelphia: Jewish Publication Society, 2010), chap. 1, https://muse.jhu.edu/book/2307.
12. Cornelius Plantinga, *Not the Way It's Supposed to Be*, 53–54.
13. Ibid., 52–53.
14. Ibid., 55.

Chapter 8: What's the Point of Suffering?

1. Paul Kalanithi, *When Breath Becomes Air* (New York: Random House, 2016), 215.
2. Ibid.
3. Ibid., 199.
4. R. C. Sproul, *Surprised by Suffering: The Role of Pain and Death in the Christian Life* (Lake Mary, FL: Ligonier Ministries, 2009), 39.
5. Jeremiah Burroughs, "Learning to Be Content," in Guthrie, *Be Still My Soul*, 163.
6. Sproul, *Surprised by Suffering*, 43.
7. Ibid., 44.
8. John Piper, "Power in Weakness," in Guthrie, *Be Still My Soul*, 150–51.
9. David Yeghnazar, "5 Ways Persecution in Iran Has Backfired," The Gospel Coalition, October 11, 2016, https://www.thegospelcoalition.org/article/5-ways-persecution-in-iran-has-backfired.
10. Ibid.
11. David Brooks, "What Suffering Does," *New York Times*, April 7, 2014, http://www.nytimes.com/2014/04/08/opinion/brooks-what-suffering-does.html.
12. Brooks, "What Suffering Does."
13. Landry Fields, "Injury Interrupted My Idolatry," Desiring God, September 26, 2015, http://www.desiringgod.org/articles/injury-interrupted-my-idolatry.
14. Ibid.
15. Ibid.
16. Lewis, *A Grief Observed*, 61.

17. Bryan Loritts, *Saving the Saved: How Jesus Saves Us from Try-Harder Christianity into Performance-Free Love* (Grand Rapids, MI: Zondervan, 2016), 139.

18. Timothy Keller, *The Reason for God: Belief in an Age of Skepticism* (New York: Dutton, 2008), 188–91.

19. Loritts, *Saving the Saved*, 146.

Chapter 9: What Happens If I'm Suffering and My Faith Isn't Enough?

1. Kate Bowler, "Death, the Prosperity Gospel and Me," *New York Times*, February 13, 2016, http://www.nytimes.com/2016/02/14/opinion/sunday/death -the-prosperity-gospel-and-me.html.

2. Ibid.

3. Ibid.

4. J. I. Packer, "Hoped-for Healing," in Guthrie, *Be Still My Soul*, 139–40.

5. Dave Furman, *Being There: How to Love Those Who Are Hurting* (Wheaton, IL: Crossway, 2016), 25.

6. Ibid.

7. Ibid., 28.

8. Ibid., 18.

9. Keller, *Walking with God*, 241.

10. Ernest Hemingway, *A Farewell to Arms*, Hemingway Library ed. (New York: Scribner, 2014), 216.

11. Keller, *Walking with God*, 250.

12. Furman, *Being There*, 126.

13. Dave Furman, "Dealing Hope in the Darkest of Nights," Desiring God, September 5, 2016, http://www.desiringgod.org/articles/dealing-hope-in-the-darkest -of-nights.

14. Ibid.

Chapter 10: What Can I Do About Suffering and Evil?

1. Ben Ellis, quoted in Russ Ramsey, "Singing Man: The Story Behind the Viral Video of Ben Ellis," The Gospel Coalition, September 26, 2016, https://www.the gospelcoalition.org/article/singing-man-story-behind-viral-video-of-ben-ellis.

2. "Hurricane Matthew: Haiti Storm Disaster Kills Hundreds," *BBC News*, October 7, 2016, http://www.bbc.com/news/world-latin-america-37582009.

3. Chris Stein, "21 Girls Kidnapped from Chibok School Released by Boko Haram, Nigeria Says," *New York Times*, October 13, 2016, https://www.nytimes .com/2016/10/14/world/africa/boko-haram-nigeria.html, and Dionne Searcy, "Years After Boko Haram Kidnapping, Dozens of Girls Are Freed, Nigeria Says," *New York Times*, May 6, 2017, https://www.nytimes.com/2017/05/06/world/africa /nigeria-boko-haram-chibok-girls.html.

4. AFP News Agency, "Drought, Hunger Add to South Sudan's Woes," *Times Live*, October 20, 2016, http://www.timeslive.co.za/africa/2016/10/20/Drought -hunger-add-to-South-Sudans-woes.

5. Merriam-Webster.com, s.v. "theology," accessed October 20, 2016, http:// www.merriam-webster.com/dictionary/theology.

6. D. A. Carson, *How Long, O Lord? Reflections on Suffering and Evil* (Grand Rapids, MI: Baker Academic, 2006), 72.

7. John Stumbo, "Suffering and Sanctification," *Alliance Life*, December 2010, n.p., http://www.cmalliance.org/alife/suffering-and-sanctification.

8. Ibid.

9. Ibid.

10. David Ireland with Louis Tharp Jr., *Letters to an Unborn Child* (New York: Harper & Row, 1974), 117–118.

After graduating from college as a theater arts major, **Bruce Bickel** entered the entertainment industry as a standup comedian. But his show-biz career was short-lived because he wasn't very funny. Like most failing comedians, he became a lawyer—a profession in which he is considered hilarious. Bruce preaches sermons quite often (but never at a church, just in his spare bedroom).

Stan Jantz has spent his entire professional career selling, publishing, and writing Christian books. Writing is his favorite book activity, because he gets to do it with his longtime coauthor, Bruce Bickel. Together Bruce and Stan have written 75 books with more than 3.5 million copies sold. They have plenty of spare time to write because neither of them has a hobby (much to the chagrin of their wives).

When he's not writing, Stan serves as the executive director of the Evangelical Christian Publishers Association. He loves this job because he gets to spend time with publishing leaders who have the audacity to think they can change the world through Christ-centered books. Stan thinks they may be on to something.

More from Bruce Bickel and Stan Jantz

Visit conversantlife.com for a complete list of their books.

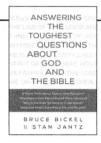

In a thoughtful, candid way, this book asks the big questions: *Is God real, and how can I know? Does God really care about me and my life?* While some answers are provided, there is enough space and grace for you to wrestle, doubt, and dig deeper.

Answering the Toughest Questions About God and the Bible

With candor, insight, and a disarming touch of humor, Bruce and Stan provide some answers to critical questions about heaven and hell, such as *What happens when you die?* and *What will heaven and hell be like?* Yet they leave enough space and grace for you to wrestle, doubt, and dig deeper.

Answering the Toughest Questions About Heaven and Hell